Diary of an Expat in Singapore

M000305758

Diary of an Expat in Singapore

Jennifer Gargiulo

Marshall Cavendish
Editions

Published by Marshall Cavendish Editions
An imprint of Marshall Cavendish International
1 New Industrial Road, Singapore 536196

Other Marshall Cavendish Offices:
Marshall Cavendish Corporation. 99 White Plains Road, Tarrytown NY 10591-
9001, USA • Marshall Cavendish International (Thailand) Co Ltd. 253 Asoke,
12th Flr, Sukhumvit 21 Road, Klongtoey Nua, Wattana, Bangkok 10110,
Thailand • Marshall Cavendish (Malaysia) Sdn Bhd, Times Subang, Lot 46,
Subang Hi-Tech Industrial Park, Batu Tiga, 40000 Shah Alam, Selangor Darul
Ehsan, Malaysia.

Marshall Cavendish is a trademark of Times Publishing Limited

National Library Board, Singapore Cataloguing-in-Publication Data:
Gargiulo, Jennifer.
Diary of an expat in Singapore / Jennifer Gargiulo. – Singapore : Marshall
Cavendish Editions, 2013.
pages cm
ISBN : 978-981-4408-57-8 (paperback)
1. Gargiulo, Jennifer – Anecdotes.   2. Aliens – Singapore – Anecdotes
3. Singapore – Social life and customs – Humor. I. Title.
JV6091
305.90691 – dc23   OCN 848549666

Printed in Singapore by Markono Print Media Pte Ltd

Contents

Preface

THIS IS NOT a diary, nor a journal. In fact, this is not even the book I wanted to write. I was thinking of some-thing more along the lines of Ernest Hemingway's 'A Moveable Feast'.

I guess this is what happens when you are not single, living in Paris, or an alcoholic. You write a blog instead. If you're incredibly lucky, an editor stumbles upon it and sees something you don't: a book.

I remember announcing the day we found out we were moving to Singapore, a country I knew nothing about: "Okay, but just one year."

That was seven years ago. Prophetic as always.

After a few months, I started recording the little things: the trivial, the dreams, the mundane. I wasn't expecting anybody to actually follow the blog, well, maybe a few readers (mostly blood relatives). Surprisingly, it started getting daily hits in the hundreds; I was pretty sure these were people googling "dumplings" or "tropical island in Southeast Asia" who had gotten there by mistake.

The one thing I've learned so far is that being an expat is more a state of mind than a location; hopefully, this book will accompany you there.

Acknowledgements

EVEN THOUGH I was the one doing the actual procrastinating and drinking coffee, I still want to thank some people who helped me along the way:

My awesome editors at Marshall Cavendish, Justin Lau and Melvin Neo, who had a vision from the very beginning and most importantly got all my jokes.

My friends, who never failed to instill fear in me by asking: "Are you finished?"

My parents, Mario and Norma, for their love and support.

My brothers, Stephen (blog statistics expert) and Julian (soul-crushing first reader).

My children, Alexander and Eliot, who never minded when I channelled my inner Oprah (usually after finishing a chapter): "You get a car! You get a car!"

And finally, my optimistic husband, Michele, who plans on retiring and living off the royalties from this book.

Diary of an Expat in Singapore

Signs you're an expat mom in Singapore

① You measure distance in taxi-minute terms.

This metric system, unique to Singapore, is very useful for those without a car. Measuring distance in taxi minutes (and more importantly, taxi dollars) can help the expat mom gauge which birthday parties her kids will be attending, and consequently, which friendships to encourage. Sleepover in JB (Johor Bahru)? I don't think so. Some friends might call this cynical but the expat mom calls it practical. One needs to follow a certain criteria when selecting friends. That's where taxis can help.

② You decide that your morning walk to drop the kids off at school is close enough to taking a bikram yoga course.

Bikram yoga is a type of yoga done in 40°C heat, a walk in Singapore is also done in 40°C heat. Throw in the 100% humidity factor and you've got yourself a party. On the plus side: walking is free. Wearing blue jeans? Not advisable. The expat mom will initially shrug off naysayers with a casual "I've seen worse." True enough, but has her hair? If her goal was looking like Marge from 'The Simpsons'... things are looking good.

❸ If you hear the term *trailing spouse* one more time...

Unless you're Wordsworth waxing lyrical about *trailing clouds of glory* in his 'Intimations of Immortality', you'd best refrain from using the term *trailing* when describing the expat mom. She's not too keen on being a trailing anything. You may refer to her as a *trailblazer.* This will go over much better. Not as much as using the words *Bali, villa,* and *rental* all in the same sentence, but far better than when she discovered the house came without a dishwasher.

❹ You'd like your children to learn Mandarin. You just don't want to be a part of it.

The expat mom has seen the characters (the many, many characters), has attended a class or two, and is well aware of what a Herculean task this is... which is why she wants no part in it. The expat mom will drop her kids off and secretly think: "Kids, you are on your own." When her kids complain about how hard it is, she will sympathize. Really. But she will still think: "Kids, you are on your own." Let's face it, if she had been meant to learn Chinese, she wouldn't have had any alcohol in college. The expat mom can be very rational when she wants to.

⑤ The only time you can wear your favourite jeans or sweater is at the movies (where it feels like winter in Alaska).

Once upon a time, the expat mom was young and adventurous. While on a stroll with her husband or kids, she may even have impulsively suggested: "Let's go to the movies." Not in Singapore, unless she wants pneumonia. The words *spontaneity* and *cinema* do not go together in Singapore. One must plan ahead and dress accordingly. Think ski trip in the Alps. Gloves optional.

⑥ Your handbag includes mosquito repellent, sunscreen, an umbrella, and your kid's bathing suit.

No self-respecting expat mom would leave the house without these essential items. You think: "For what... the jungle?" The expat mom thinks: "Hmmm no, suburban Singapore." Mentally she imagines an episode of 'Man vs. Wild' and prepares for the worst. You say: "Picnic on the East Coast," she hears: "Dengue fever." You say: "Drizzling," she hears: "Tropical rainstorm." And if you say: "Lounge by the pool," she hears: "Sunburn." And yes, it is selective hearing.

⑦ You discover a bottle of wine costs as much as a mini vacation.

The allure of living in exotic Southeast Asia drops dramatically the very first time the expat mom goes shopping. Forget the Chardonnay she was accustomed to... she might very well be drinking Tang from now on. On the plus side, this might be the only country where getting a shrink is actually cheaper than drowning your sorrows in wine. I can't imagine the alcoholism rate is high. Do Singaporeans not drink wine? With such exorbitant prices (multiply by ten if you are planning to drink outside the home, at say an actual bar or restaurant), drinking is prohibitive. There really is no such thing as a *casual* drink out with friends... at that price tag, consider it an investment.

8 You miss your car, your best friend, your relatives. In that order.

The fact that owning a Toyota Corolla here costs as much as owning a Porsche 911 elsewhere should be a good indicator of whether you and your family will be acquiring a car. Not likely. The fact that the exorbitant tax levy is actually a bit of urban planning genius doesn't really soften the blow. Nor the realization that this is what keeps pollution and gridlock at bay. It should, but it doesn't. Not when you have to carry groceries in the rain.

And the spouse employee should make no mistake: should the company decide to cough up a car, guess who will be using it? Sure, if you're lucky, she might drop you off at the office after leaving the kids at school. But after work, during rush hour? You're on your own. After all, you were always boasting about the amazing public transportation system.

9 You know the difference between a gecko and a lizard.

Not really something the expat mom can add to her c.v. but impressive nonetheless. It does smack of Southeast Asia insider information. Newsflash: This is the only reptile she will ever be happy to see in the house. Of course, if it's jumping out of the fridge when she's reaching for maple syrup it might spook her. What? The air con wasn't high enough?

10 You become an expert at dealing with jet lag.

There is nobody, and I mean nobody, better at dealing with jet lag than the expat mom. She could hold a TED conference on the subject... she's that good. You may think that's because nobody really needs this particular talent... really? When your toddler is demanding breakfast at 2 a.m., who are you going to call?

11 You don't fight with your kids so much... but that could be because you don't hear them over the construction work.

There is a reason you have the number of the NEA (National Environment Agency) taped to your refrigerator. And it's not because your husband works there. The good news is the NEA will dispatch a car to get the construction site to shut down the drilling because it's theoretically illegal after 11 pm. The bad news is the overseer suffers from short-term memory loss and you will need to call again the next day. And the next.

⑫ At $12 a box, you classify Cheerios as a luxury item.

Forget oysters and foie gras. The expat mom may be depressed at first to discover that in Singapore cereal costs as much as salmon. She will come around. Breakfast is, after all, the most important meal of the day. There is no better time to follow local customs: "Kids, here's your porridge." If it's good enough for Goldilocks...

⑬ You disregard the humidity index of 100% and think a picnic at the Botanic Gardens is a good idea.

The Botanic Gardens is an oasis in the middle of the city. Think lily pads, walking trails, rare orchids. A picnic in the middle of the day? Eliot's face says it best:

"Lovely day for a picnic."

Signs you're an expat dad in Singapore

① Your children's international school fees leave you fairly disconcerted ($33,000 for third grade... what are they learning, rocket science?).

There are some expats who don't know how much their children's school fees are. That's because their fees are covered by the company in what is reverently called the *expat package*. These are the lucky expats. You are not one of them.

Some dads dream at night of all the wonderful things their kids are learning at school. You have insomnia. Seeing your child play Minecraft doesn't help.

When the expat dad first arrived, he was surprised to discover Singaporeans are not allowed to attend international schools. In this way, the government is protecting its students and avoiding any possibility of elitism by ensuring that every Singaporean has an equal opportunity and a vested interest in keeping the public school system competitive. Or, as one (possibly paranoid) taxi driver confided, it is a great way to track students from the first grade onwards. The government even awards the best students scholarships to study at foreign universities, the only condition being their commitment to return to work for Singapore. This avoids a brain drain (such as other countries experience). It's like the U.S. Army ROTC... minus the push-ups.

When the expat dad discovers this competitive educational system comes at about $5 per month, he might break down. There may be some sobbing involved.

② Your kids boast about staying in 5-star resorts. Your childhood often involved a tent.

One of the perks of living in Southeast Asia is the plethora of amazing places at your doorstep: pristine beaches, lush rainforests, and exotic cities. Pretty soon the expat dad sees this more as a liability than a perk. Especially since his expat wife and family are quickly making the switch from modest hotels to luxury resorts. Initially, it's because the drinking water is safe. Afterwards, it's the champagne buffets and water sports in gorgeous waters. And, if you thought drinking alcohol in Singapore was prohibitive, try Bali.

③ You welcome 11 pm conference calls with California... not really.

For the working and non-working spouse alike, maintaining relationships with the United States is tough. Tougher than Europe. Blame it on the 12-hour time difference. Travelling there and back is no picnic either. The 24-hour trip is nothing compared to the massive jet lag, which will hit you like a sledgehammer. Throw in a couple of toddlers and it's a party.

④ Business trips are fine... unless they involve a Sunday.

There is nothing the expat spouse likes less than having the working spouse out of town on the weekend. During the week, it's fine, almost routine. Early dinners with the kids, late-night snacks in front of the TV, no fighting over the remote... but Sunday, that's another story. Nobody should be alone with the kids for that long.

⑤ Your wife keeps close track of your frequent flyer miles.

Similar to the way the expat mom measures distance in taxi dollars (the restaurant is about $6 away – during peak hour), plane trips are assessed in frequent flyer currency. For example, should the expat dad need to go on a business trip to Boston in January, he thinks: "It's going to be freezing." She reasons: "That's 70,000 points... totally worth it." She may not have been so strong in math before, but now she's sharp as a whip.

⑥ You know which Asian airport has the best lounge, best sushi, longest taxi queue.

As a seasoned business traveller, the expat dad is more adept than Jason Bourne at navigating airports (without a concealed weapon, of course). In fact, he probably knows the airports better than the cities he's going to. And, of course, this makes the expat dad that much happier when he lands at Changi, Singapore's international airport. Dorothy in 'The Wizard of Oz' said: "There's no place like home." The expat dad will secretly chant: "There's no place like Changi."

⑦ You could be playing golf or relaxing by the pool but you're not doing much of either.

Expat dads dream of playing golf in Malaysia and lounging by the pool. In reality, they're either recovering from jet lag, going to the chiropractor for their backs, or trying to re-negotiate the 100% rental increase on their condo lease. The latter being the most stressful as there is rarely an upgrade or maintenance done to justify the raise. The fun bit comes when the agent inspects the apartment before you hand it back to your landlord. You realize the things you never complained about when you got the apartment because you didn't want to be an annoying tenant (the broken closet shelf, the faulty stove burner...) are now all your fault. And, you need to pay for them. Remember that deposit? Good luck with that. If one were paranoid, it would be legitimate to suspect apartments in Singapore are rented out with the sole purpose of renovating them with the tenants' forfeited deposit once the tenants have left. Luckily the expat dad is too tired to be paranoid.

8 Your wife no longer asks who the best-looking women are but she has noticed you whistle when you pack for Tokyo.

This may be just a consequence of the many stylish Japanese women the expat wife sees around the condo. More likely, it's from hearing them protest: "Us... beautiful and stylish? Noooo – you should see the women in Tokyo." Before each trip, the expat dad should expect to be reminded how bossy Japanese wives are.

Signs you're an expat kid in Singapore

1 **Your parents don't ground you. They threaten to turn off the air conditioning.**

When I first arrived in Singapore, I had a friend who used this method of discipline. No yelling or caning necessary. When her two sons were mucking about at bedtime, the simple threat of turning off the air con would apparently strike the fear of God in them. I knew I had a true expat kid when threatening to turn off the air conditioning had a more immediate effect than not allowing him to go out and play with friends. A true expat kid will always place air con above friendships.

2 **When you meet a friend for the first time, you ask them: "How big is your pool?"**

Also known as the expat kid ice-breaker, this question can be a great conversation-opener. All over the world, kids meeting for the first time ask each other what grade they are in. Not in Singapore. The expat kid cuts straight to the chase. This may or may not be intended as a way to gauge the true size of a pool. After all, we are in a country where most condos boast their own pool (an extravagant, unheard-of luxury in cities such as New York or Verona, Italy, where I come from). If you still haven't broken it to your expat kid that in most places people don't really discuss the size of their pools (any more than they would the size of their bank accounts), don't worry, you have time. The departure lounge at Changi Airport might be a good place. In the meantime, let him relish being in hot and tropical Singapore, where most play dates involve a pool, and where a bathing suit is casually tossed inside mom's handbag. Clearly there is truth to the claim that a pool is an extension of the expat kid. Now, about those swimming lessons.

❸ You complain that there is something you don't like about the kindergarten class. (It's the Mandarin.)

This one is dear to my heart. When we first arrived in Singapore, like all expats I had just two priorities: not dying of heat stroke and having my kids become fluent in Chinese. Just kidding (about the heat stroke part).

In my supreme ignorance, I assumed I would sign my son up for soccer or basketball and he would just naturally pick up the local language. Wrong. Singaporean kids do not speak Chinese. Or let me rephrase that: they may indeed speak Chinese with their parents at home, but they don't speak it amongst themselves. And, even if they do, they most certainly won't speak it with you, an *angmoh* (literally this term means 'redhead', but is used to indicate all expats). After all, they speak English, so why make the extra effort?

Luckily for the Mandarin-hungry expat parent, most schools offer Chinese. The Montessori school that Alexander was accepted to when we first arrived had an unusual session: 12:30 to 3:30 pm. At first, I thought it was a joke since for most Italian mothers of a three-year-old that time is reserved for lunch followed by a nap. Now it meant heading out in the midday heat (no joke in Singapore, where the sun is beating down so hard at that hour you could fry an egg on your head). Two of these days were dedicated to Chinese. The *laoshi* didn't speak any English, which was amazing... for me. For Alexander, not so much. Unable to articulate at first what was wrong (maybe the jet lag hadn't passed yet), Alexander would merely say: "I know it's the same classroom and the same kids... but there's just something I don't like about it." Hmm, the Chinese? I wondered guiltily to myself.

It must be said that learning Chinese is the bane of all expat kids' existence. Well, it couldn't be all fun and games now, could it?

④ A plane ride any shorter than ten hours leaves you disappointed. "That's all?"

Unlike most children, the expat kid is used to travelling at least yearly to a very faraway place referred to as *home*.

The expat kid is not sure why this faraway place is referred to as *home*, since everything commonly denoting a home – his bed, teddy bear, comic book collection – is, as far as he is concerned, already at *home* in Singapore. However, he is not only used to the long plane rides, he craves them. After all, it's the only place where he can watch six movies back to back, uninterrupted. And, if his mother dozes off, one of those movies can be 'Runaways', a rock-and-roll bio of Joan Jett. Appropriate for an eight-year-old? Not really.

⑤ Roti prata and seasoned seaweed are your favourite snacks.

Pretty self-explanatory. Expat kids love roti prata – flat bread dipped into fishhead curry. You might want to omit the *fishhead* part when you first introduce it to them. I've seen Singaporeans and Indian vendors alike surprised at my kids' tolerance for hot, spicy curry.

The seaweed I blame on the strong Japanese influence in the snacks department here in Singapore. The wide array of rice crackers, barbecued seaweed, and cute packaging at grocery stores are just *kawaii* (irresistible). At least one of the reasons it's so nice to have Japanese kids over on playdates: you never know what treat they will bring over. This holds true for kindergarten – once they start Kumon you won't be seeing them so much.

⑥ You think the corner on the sidewalk outside your condo is for hailing taxis.

You mean the corner on the sidewalk in front of your condo isn't for hailing taxis? Let's see, if you're an expat kid who leaves the condo (a.k.a. Mormon compound) only on a school bus, then I can see your quandary. Why else would you go there? You have never actually gone on a walk outside the condo. If your parents don't own a car, you will indeed be taking a lot of taxis. The expat kid will take to this like a fish takes to water. It will become second nature. And, the prospect of even a five-minute walk will seem daunting and warrant the request: "Shouldn't we take a taxi? There's a green one coming now." Green refers to the green light on top of the taxi's windshield and theoretically denotes a vacant taxi. I use the term *theoretically* because the driver ultimately has the last word. It is not uncommon for the taxi driver to lower his window, hear where you have to go, shake his head violently no and drive off. Thus leaving you feeling only slightly less rejected than when you used to stand in your middle school cafeteria looking for a place to sit.

The expat kid's love of the taxi will become more controversial when you're back 'home', where one only takes taxis to airports and hospitals. The fact that the taxi driver 'home' is wearing a Rolex should give you a clue as to why that is.

⑦ You dream about wearing gloves and sweaters.

The expat kid craves cold weather. At least he thinks he does, having never actually experienced it. He dreams of wind, ice, sleet, and frost. Above all else, he dreams of snow. In the expat kid's mind, snow is the one thing missing from his life. The reason for this: snowball fights.

⑧ When they find a cobra at your school, you reassure your mother: "It was just a little one."

When you were at school, your field trip may have been to the museum to see a documentary on the rainforest in Malaysia. The expat kid's field trip is to the actual rainforest in Malaysia. Nothing fazes him. He wears mosquito patches at the playground against dengue fever, carries a water bottle in case of a sudden drought, and he's probably seen a cobra in the school drain. And, even if it's a little one, we are still using the term *cobra*. You sometimes wonder if the expat kid is really a kid or a Navy Seal in training.

⑨ When you don't see your Dad at home, you wonder if he's in China or Japan.

Most kids who don't see their dads (or moms, if she's the working spouse) at the dinner table might ask: "Where is Dad/Mom?" Not the expat kid. He asks if he's in China or Japan – hoping the latter because that's where all the cool toys come from.

**⑩ You've probably travelled in business class
at least once. Your parents realize
this was a huge mistake.**

It usually works like this: in expat households all over
Singapore, one spouse travels while the other calculates
air miles. The working spouse hears "New York," and
thinks of the 24 hours he'll be spending on planes. The
air-mile spouse hears "New York," and thinks of free trips,
upgrades, and stays at the Sheraton. The expat kid hears
"New York," and asks: "Are we travelling business?"

Politically incorrect expat profiling

1 Swedes: Most likely to be training for a triathlon.

The Swedish expat does not have a maid, swims in icy waters, builds his own house, and spends an inordinate amount of time in saunas drinking pure grain alcohol. He may or may not have invented Ikea. Swedes like spending their afternoon with the kids there (whether they need to buy something or not) and are especially proud of the meatballs sold at the canteen. If you accompany them on a fun outing to Ikea (how do you spell oxymoron?), you will be expected to eat them as well. This was before the horse meat incident. Should you bring the Swedish mom in your condo soup for her sick child, prepare to wait a bit... as she sends you home with a batch of cinnamon buns... she just cooked from scratch.

② Persians: Most likely to be marinating lamb chops in Manolo Blahniks.

Most popular at condo barbecues and potlucks, the Persian expat knows his meat. And no pull-out sofa for their guests – they put them up at the ritziest hotel in town. For the Persian expat, Bintan is roughing it. If you are invited over for dinner: dress up. And don't forget a sleeping bag for the kids – it's going to be late.

③ Italians: Most likely to be carrying sweaters.

People credit the beautiful Italian scarf industry to expert craftsmanship... actually, it's their fear of drafts. Upon entering a room, the Italian expat is prone to inquire: "Can you turn the air con off?" The Italian expat is, on the one hand, happy to find *pandoro* (traditional Christmas cake) here in Singapore, on the other hand, slightly aghast to discover it costs 20 times as much as at home. Unrelated, the Italian expat wonders why Singaporeans like their noodles overcooked.

4 Brits: Most likely to talk about the weather.

Not all Brits discuss the weather, go to the British Club, and watch soccer. That's a gross exaggeration... I know at least one who prefers field hockey.

Full disclosure: When I first arrived in Singapore, I wanted to send my children to the British School. And yes, it was just so they could get a British accent. I am that shallow. But who else can make the word *butter* sound so posh? A doorman in England sounds more cultivated than a professor at Harvard.

5 Irish: Most likely to be playing rugby.

Not even microsporidia (awful parasite lurking in the muddy fields after rain) will discourage the Irish expat from having his kids play rugby. Italians wouldn't think of going near a field with that sort of potential danger. But the Irish expat is not totally unprepared... hence the eye drops.

I have to admit to a soft spot for Ireland. Maybe it's because I lived in Dublin years ago, as a first-time mom, above Bewley's on Westmoreland Street. My almost pathological love for the city is probably viewed suspiciously even (especially) by my Irish expat friends. I just can't help it. Oscar Wilde, Yeats (both brothers, the poet and the painter), James Joyce, Father Ted, Graham Norton, Guinness, the different types of rain. I love it all. Especially the sense of humour. To this day, when I think how my Irish expat friend, Therese, after being told a long and confusing story, whispered to me, "Well, there's seven-and-a-half minutes I'm never getting back," I can't stop smiling.

⑥ Japanese: Most likely to be wearing large hats.

It took me about two years of living in my condo to realize that I was either living in downtown Tokyo or that I was in a Japanese-listed condo. It was the latter.

One thing you notice when living with the Japanese is how seriously they take sun protection. Forget about wearing wide-brimmed hats outdoors, if you really want to be Japanese, wear long gloves on the tennis court.

⑦ Indians: Most likely to be comparing schools.

The Indian expat launches websites, compares ways to best store a sari in Singapore, and discusses the heat in Mumbai. Expect lengthy discussions on where to buy gold, the benefits of eating paneer, and whether or not to get PR (Permanent Residence).

⑧ Singaporeans: Most likely to be indoors studying.

The Singaporean, not an expat per se, since this is after all her country, is too much an integral part of the expat's life to not be included. First of all, do not expect to see Singaporean kids around the condo. If you do meet a mom, she is very likely carrying a heavy textbook to brush up on her math before tutoring her child. If it is the PSLE (Primary School Leaving Exam) time of year, you won't see her for weeks. Do not feel rejected. Remember when she told you she only moved to this condo because it was within the one-kilometre range of the primary school she wanted her child to attend? She wasn't joking.

⑨ Aussies: Most likely to be throwing shrimp on the barbie.

Whether it's having a glass of wine al fresco or organizing barbecues, the Aussie expat knows how to have a good time. Voted most likely to wear flip-flops at the Raffles Hotel, the expat from Down Under is the definition of informal. Just don't try to compare the beaches in Southeast Asia with those in Australia. And never ask him if he's been on an episode of 'Bondi Rescue'. Steer clear of coffee as well. When in doubt, tell him Australia is your Plan B... he'll understand.

Stuff
first-time visitors
to Singapore say

❶ "It's like being on vacation."

There is nobody more enthusiastic about Singapore than the first-time visitor. As he lays by your pool in December, the grey skies and chilly winds he left behind a distant memory, he will think he died and went to heaven. Then a jackhammer breaks the idyllic silence and the only one speaking in a normal tone of voice is you. Later, as he watches you put a mosquito patch on your child before heading to the playground, he might ask: "Dengue? What's dengue?" His enthusiasm will noticeably wane from that moment on.

❷ "Is it always so hot here?"

It is day three and severe dehydration has set in. The crippling jet lag has made the first-time visitor grouchy. Fighting a strong urge to flee to Changi Airport, he decides that he doesn't actually care for the weather as much as he originally thought he did. It's too darn hot. And, the fact that last night he invited you out for drinks and after graciously picking up the tab realized he wiped out his entire trip's budget... doesn't help.

③ "It doesn't look like it's going to rain."

When the first-time visitor comes back home dripping wet because he refused to take the umbrella you offered and couldn't find a taxi, resist the temptation to mumble: "I told you so." According to Dante, no other words in the spoken language hurt quite as much. If you value your friendship, refrain. Gently remind the visitor that in Singapore it is advisable to carry an umbrella regardless of how the sky looks.

"I don't need an umbrella."

④ "Why is the air con on all the time?"

The first-time visitor views air con disparagingly. An unnecessary luxury. He secretly thinks: "I would never waste all that money on electricity. I would just keep the windows open and enjoy the breeze." He is still blissfully unaware that any breeze that comes in feels like a *scirocco* from the Sahara.

⑤ "Can you turn the air con on?!"

It is day five and the visitor's body has still not fully acclimatized. The street is too hot, the shade by the pool is too hot, the visitor is just too hot. He now knows there is only one thing that can take him out of his misery: air conditioning. Just pass him the remote control and point to the snowflake.

⑥ "I love walking."

The visitor professes a love for walking second to none. He may very well have strolled down the cobblestoned streets of London and the tree-lined boulevards of Paris, but he has never walked through the CBD (Central Business District) at noon. To avoid dampening his enthusiasm, do not let on at first that Singapore isn't really a walking city. Just send him to one of the city's many parks. MacRitchie Reservoir, for example. Sure it has ravenous monkeys but what's the alternative? City walking? Not unless you want heat stroke. Soon enough, the wannabe walking visitor will ask: "Or should we maybe take a taxi?"

⑦ "If I had a pool, I would always be by the pool."

Don't argue, let him figure this one out on his own. Do not point out that there is a reason swimming pools are deserted most of the day (and no, you are not counting the tanning Finns). It's not just the sudden noxious fumes of mosquito fogging or the nearby earsplitting drilling. So, while I agree that the possibility of having a pool is by far the most awesome part of the expat life in Singapore, will you find me lying by one? No. Do I want a stroke? Not especially. You will find me in the shade wearing a wide-brimmed hat (and what my husband calls my *burkhini*) with my Japanese posse, doing what Japanese do best by the pool: watching their kids have a swimming lesson.

After a few hours by the pool, the first-time visitor will suggest going inside in no uncertain terms. "I am dying out here," he might think to himself. If he forgot to put on sunscreen, claiming, "Oh, I'm lucky like that, I never get burned" – two words: aloe vera. The industrial size.

⑧ "I love local food."

You thought you loved local food. But you were wrong. Nobody likes local food more than the first-time visitor. Not even the locals themselves. He scoffs at your food choices and demands: "More chili, please." The visitor explores with gusto hawker centres and wet markets looking for something original and genuine. Until something bothers him, like chopsticks. "Where is the fork? I can't eat with chopsticks. This is ridiculous."

⑨ **"Everything is so cheap here."**

One trip to the supermarket should dispel that myth.

Signs you're in a taxi in Singapore

"You talkin' to me?"

① The driver turns without signalling.

Most expats have a love-hate relationship with taxis. Probably because it is slightly perplexing and vexing that although taxis are everywhere, this does not mean you will actually get one. In fact, it's all pretty arbitrary. You try to flag down a taxi. The driver may or may not slow down, may or may not agree to take you where you need to go, and may or may not reach the agreed destination. The whole process is arbitrary.

② Kids call the driver *uncle*.

As long as the driver doesn't call me *sister*, I don't really have a problem with this. It's a Singaporean thing, the cleaning lady is an *auntie*, the taxi driver is an *uncle*. It's like the whole island is related. Worse than a Mafia wedding.

③ The driver expects you to tell him how to get where you need to go.

In other countries, it's the exact opposite. You take a taxi because you don't know how to get where you need to go. Not in Singapore. You'd better know exactly where you need to go, how to get there, and whether to take the PIE, CTE, AYE… no, it's not a game of Scrabble, but acronyms for the different routes you can take: PIE (Pan-Island Expressway, the oldest and longest expressway), CTE (Central Expressway), and AYE (Ayer Rajah Expressway). Soon you'll be saying, "Just take the AYE to avoid the ERP," with the best of them. Btw, if any urban planners are reading this: the ERP (automatic Electronic Road Pricing)? Not very popular.

④ There is a pretty good chance you will have your wallet returned.

I think it's safe to say that anywhere in the world, forgetting valuables in a cab is not a good thing. It's tantamount to kissing them goodbye. Here, it is not surprising to see someone breathe a sigh of relief: "Oh, I just left it in the taxi this morning." Like that's a good thing. And, it often is. A taxi driver famously returned $1.1 million left behind by a Thai couple. What they were doing with that much cash in the first place was never discovered. My guess is they were going to buy cheese (see 'Signs you're not slumming it in Singapore').

⑤ You feel lucky.

Why? Because this means you actually managed to flag one down. Most likely after three other taxis drove away, vigorously shaking their heads *no* after you told them where you needed to go. And, even though they say it's because they are at the end of their shift (really... at 11:30 am?), their refusal still stings.

⑥ You're feeling *really* lucky.

Why? Because it's raining outside. And no, it's not just an impression. There really are fewer taxis around when it's raining... you know, when you need them most. Whether it's for insurance or spite, nobody can confirm. Surely, this doesn't endear taxi drivers to commuters. At least, not in a downpour.

Signs you're at a Starbucks in Singapore

① It's colder than the average Starbucks.

Starbucks is ubiquitous and Singapore is no exception. Same logo, same coffee, just colder. Madonna claimed: "Italians do it better." Singapore's Tourism Board should claim: "We do it colder."

When I ask my Singaporean friends why they would agree to pay $6 for a cup of coffee when they could get it at a kopitiam for $2, they answer without hesitation: "It's not about the coffee. It's the lifestyle. You're paying for the air con, the cool soundtrack, the free Wi-Fi."

② They sell green tea chai lattes.

If Singapore is going to carry international chains then those chains had better be localized if they want to be successful. Hence, the green tea chai latte at Starbucks, the prosperity chicken burgers at McDonald's, and the spicy toppings at Pizza Hut.

Did anybody see my coffee?

③ There are textbooks spread out on every table.

Judging from the many students, textbooks strewn about, and nervous looks, it would appear Starbucks is the number one destination when cramming for exams.

④ The staff speaks Malay.

I have been to many Starbucks around the island and the staff is almost always Malay. I have no idea why this is. On their own coffee breaks, they choose spicy nasi lemak rather than blueberry muffins, but when it comes to grinding coffee, they know their beans.

**⑤ If it's Chinese New Year, with every purchase
of a venti size beverage, you will receive
a pack of *hong bao* (red packets).**

Hong bao are the little red packets containing crisp, new,
even-numbered banknotes that are given to friends and
relatives on Chinese New Year for good luck. *Hong bao* is
also a word that brings joy to every Singaporean kid and
every expat kid who follows local traditions. Strangely
enough, my own kids profess a sudden affinity for all
things Chinese just around this time of year. Forget the
tooth fairy, they're looking for their *hong bao*. The tooth
fairy is an unreliable late-night visitor but *hong bao* are a
certainty.

**⑥ If it is the Year of the Snake, the teddy bear
sold at Starbucks will have a
snake on its shoulder.**

Children always want teddy bears, and when they walk
into Starbucks it's no different. Only difference is that if
you're in Singapore, and it happens to be the year of the
snake, the teddy bear will have a reptile draped over its
shoulders. The fact that it is stuffed and made of green
velveteen makes it only slightly less creepy. But if it brings
good luck, who cares if a snake isn't exactly the cuddliest
or most desirable animal for a toddler to hug at bedtime?

Stuff
expat moms
in Singapore say

① "I love the weather here."

The weather is the great divide. You either love it or hate it. Humidity is where the buck stops. There are those who initially hate the constant heat and fear they will never wear their favourite jeans again and then grow to love it.

② "I hate the weather here."

You may look at the blue skies from your window and think: "What a beautiful day for a walk outside." Big mistake. Once you leave your air-conditioned apartment and open the front door, and the hot air sucks the breath out of you and envelopes you like an electric blanket, you realize that (1) it was your mind playing tricks on you, and (2) it's going to be a very short walk.

❸ "I miss the seasons."

The changing of seasons is at the top of all expats' list of things they miss from back home. For my kids, who have lived here most their lives, the seasons are almost an abstract concept. It is very hard for them to understand the statement: "It's cold in December." "Really, cold? Then why is the air con on?" Sometimes, I feel guilty that I'm depriving them of all the glorious autumns, springs, and winters I experienced as a kid. Then again, they'll probably never have frostbite or have to shovel a driveway... guilt gone.

I don't miss winter all that much.

❹ "Do you have a maid?"

Whether you have a maid, have had a maid, or ever contemplated getting a maid, be prepared to hear this topic... a lot. Young vs old? Well, you don't want a late-night partier but you don't want someone with arthritis either. And the discussion doesn't end there: Filipina, Indonesian, or from Myanmar (in other words: speaks English, acts *like* she speaks English, or really has no idea what you are saying)? Live-in or part-time? Maids provide a never-ending supply of conversation fodder. For example, revealing one's maid's nickname is Slow Mo (as in slow motion) because she washes salad so slowly she gets to know the leaves on a first-name basis, or complaining at a social gathering about how one's maid always talks on the phone, will bond two expats quicker than coming from the same town. When expats without help meet, they smile with a complicit air of superiority. Kind of like when people who decide to home-school meet... but without the glazed look.

⑤ "Should I get my hair rebonded?"

Like maids, the topic of whether or not to get one's hair rebonded (chemically straightened) acquires marked relevancy in a country as challenging to Western-style hair as Singapore. Pros and cons are discussed at length on expat forums. If you have gravity-defying curly hair like mine that grows visibly higher every step you take outside, you might be tempted. Just remember, it's only temporary.

⑥ "I'm thinking of getting a car."

I don't drive. So when I hear my expat friends talk about how much they miss their cars, how it was an extension of their house, complete with snacks, toys, and change of clothes... I can't really relate. The closest I ever came to owning a vehicle was when I had a baby stroller.

⑦ "Don't even think about getting a car."

In Singapore, it's cheaper to take taxis and they're plentiful. Just stay positive when you happen to be waiting under the rain with your kids and two green-lighted (supposedly vacant) taxis pass you by. The first claims he's only taking passengers to Jurong, while the second is waving his arm so frenetically he seems to be waging war with a bee.

⑧ "My husband is in... (fill in the blank)."

The expat mom is living in Singapore. The working spouse... not so much. China, India, Japan – really depends on the week. There is a lot of travelling and conjugal separation in the expat's domestic life. Get used to it. You'll be alone a lot. On the plus side, no more fighting over what to watch on TV. On the negative, if you slip and break your foot (true story)... you're on your own. Additional tip: Keep the number of a good plumber handy.

⑨ "Are you going home for the summer?"

Initially expats go home for winter and summer, then just summer, until one day they wonder: "Wouldn't it be cheaper to go to the Maldives?"

⑩ "Isn't Singapore Airlines great?"

Once upon a time, the expat mom looked for great flight bargains over the internet. Five-hour layover in Doha? No problem. But once she flies Singapore Airlines... there's just no turning back. It has been said that flying Singapore

Airlines means your holiday starts as soon as you board the plane (Okay, I said it). Even when I had a baby strapped to my waist and a toddler with constant requests, I still clocked in about four movies while balancing a glass of chardonnay on my knee. That's just the kind of multi-tasker I am. When it comes to watching movies I can be pretty ruthless. Being an adult can be great. If you're flying Singapore Airlines... it's awesome. And no, I do not work for them. Yet.

11 "I love Bali."

All expat moms love Bali. They've either just been there, want to go there, want to rent a villa with their visiting relatives there, or stay at a boutique resort amongst the rice paddies in Ubud. Exotic Bali is the go-to place for Singapore expats. You don't know what to do on your next break? Go to Bali. Your relatives are coming? Go to Bali. It's your honeymoon, wedding anniversary, 40th birthday... *go to Bali!*

12 "Lombok is the way Bali used to be."

As soon as the expat mom reserves her tickets for Bali, the first person she meets will say: "Bali? You should go to Lombok. It's the way Bali used to be." On a scale of one to ten, this will annoy the expat mom about a ten. Especially since she will hear that exact same thing from about ten different and totally random people. Suddenly her hair-dresser, the taxi driver, the cashier at the grocery store are all experts on Lombok. "But I thought Bali..." you will try to say. "No," they will mock you. "Bali is so last year. You really should have chosen Lombok." And, you really *should* go to Lombok. As long as you realize that as soon as you buy your tickets, they will say: "Lombok? You should go to Bhutan."

More stuff expat moms in Singapore say

① "I read it in the Straits Times."

The expat mom may read the local newspaper but she has the front page of her newspaper from back home as her browser homepage. This serves different purposes. She already knows what the weather is like when her mom calls, she can see how cheap books are back home, and how her favourite soccer team fared over the weekend. It's a good way to keep up with the gossip about those home-town starlets and disgraced politicians that never feature in the Straits Times.

② "Singapore is so safe."

Like almost all stereotypes this one is both true and annoying all at once, especially for Singaporeans. I'm sure that just hearing it makes them want to reach for a can of mace and spray it in your face. In fact, though incredibly grateful to live in a safe city, the expat mom will never say this to a local resident. It's because she fears that if she does they'll want to punch her on the spot. She's probably right. The thing she would really like to know is why she never sees any police around or hears any sirens. But she doesn't ask... just in case she's talking to a plainclothes cop.

③ "Where do your kids go to school? Is that fee per year or... life?"

Expat moms allegedly ask this question to know if their children know each other. The truth is that misery loves company. Sure, the school is amazing, has a state-of-the-art theatre, an Olympic swimming pool, the whole deal; she just wasn't aware that her child's education would cost as much as a second mortgage on the house.

④ "My kids have mycoplasma."

If you are an expat in Singapore, chances are you're going to be treated for mycoplasma. Whether you actually have it, that's another story. Mycoplasma is a word the expat mom never even heard of before coming to Singapore. Now it's mycoplasma this, mycoplasma that. Whenever a kid coughs, sneezes, or looks drowsy, somebody will say: "He may have mycoplasma." Elsewhere, it's just a common cold that requires hot soup, fluids, and rest. Not here. The doctor dangles the word in front of the expat mom. "There is a test for it but the results take a while, so why don't we go ahead and treat it as though it were mycoplasma?" The doctor will then hand her a prescription for Klacid (a special $150 antibiotic), and may even absentmindedly point to the cash machine as he says this. In honour of the Ponzi scheme, I like to call this the Mycoplasma scheme. In other countries they steal your wallet, here they diagnose you with mycoplasma. Seriously, how many people could possibly have walking pneumonia at the same time?

When the expat mom's child, back home in Verona for the summer, gets pneumonia, the expat mom is flabbergasted when she buys the antibiotic from her pharmacist: $5. "But it's Klacid. This costs more than gold in Singapore." Lesson to be learned: (1) It's better to be a pharmacist in Singapore? (2) Only get pneumonia in Italy? Or: (3) When the diagnosis is mycoplasma, get a second opinion? The correct answer? All of the above.

Fun fact: When the expat mom also gets pneumonia in Italy and hers is the bad, bacterial kind which requires a three-day hospitalization, the entire bill will add up to the cost of one box of Klacid back in Singapore. She may have to share her room with four octogenarians, and go without a TV and air con, but who cares? Forget writing... she should be selling Klacid instead.

⑤ "My kids need more Mandarin."

The expat mom knows her kids need more Mandarin. The reason she knows this is that they still sing the same two songs they learned three years ago in kindergarten and look completely baffled when taxi drivers ask them questions. The issue is *how much more*?

Normally understanding and sympathetic, the expat mom will be unusually heartless when it comes to tracking her child's progress in Mandarin. She has been known to threaten: "That's it, only cartoons in Mandarin from now on."

Forget good looks and fast cars, the one who knows the phone number of a good Mandarin tutor holds the key to the expat mom's heart.

6 "If I lived in a house I would definitely get a dog."

Right. And, since all kids want a dog, the expat mom has no choice but to remove any possibility of that actually happening, however remote. For example, renouncing PR, which is the only way she could buy a landed house. She will say the renunciation is so her son doesn't one day have to do National Service duty (two-year military obligation which would actually be good for him), but really it is to eliminate the possibility of getting landed property, hence a dog. Even though expats can't buy landed houses they can rent them. Sure, it might be a more pleasant environment for a dog but the Ferraris and Porsches parked outside are a good indicator of what bank account you'll need to live in one.

7 "When did you get back?"

The expat mom is generally in a state of flux. Most likely she has just returned from a trip home, a holiday, or a 'go see' for her next location. Trips involve different time zones. All involve jet lag. Descartes claimed: "I think, therefore I am." The expat mom would change that to: "I travel, therefore I am... jet-lagged." Those who have chosen to not travel during the holidays find comfort in the uncomely sight of their terribly, almost clinically, jet-lagged friends. This inevitably makes them feel better about their decision to stay put.

⑧ "My husband is learning Mandarin... Please, let this not mean we are moving to China."

This is a red flag – do not ignore it. Short of leaving a huge sign on the dining table with the words, "We are moving to China," the fact that your husband is studying Chinese (and not complaining about it) is as clear a sign as any you are going to get. Statements like "Shanghai is such a vibrant city" and "Beijing has so much to offer" should also set off warning bells.

Signs
you may have
overstayed

**① When someone asks the kids where they're
from, they answer Singapore.**

Sometimes, I'm afraid we've stayed too long in Southeast
Asia and that the kids won't know their roots. What those
roots are I'm not exactly sure. Alexander and Eliot were
both born in Verona, but their father (a Veronese) claims
they will never be true *Veronesi* – he's basing this on the
fact that they don't swear, play soccer, or eat horse meat.
So, I guess this means, for better or worse, Singapore is
their home. But sometimes I get nervous. What if they
never fit in when we do return to live in Italy (whenever
that may be)? The traits they've recently acquired do nothing to assuage my fears.

② The craving to eat hot, spicy chicken at 10 am.

Singaporeans used to openly stare at my young daughter dipping flat prata bread nonchalantly in hot fishhead

curry sauce. Roti prata remains her favourite meal to this day along with curry noodles, but spicy chicken is a close second. If we were still in Verona, they might be eating a croissant at 10 am. But after growing up in Singapore... it's spicy food.

③ Alexander's familiarity with chopsticks.

I love watching my son eat with chopsticks. My husband? Less so. I can't help but feel he's trying to show off. An Italian friend visiting us wondered why Asians still use chopsticks. "It's not like they haven't *seen* a fork?" Of course, he may have just been grumpy because he was starving in front of a plate of delicious chili crab unable to use his chopsticks. The crab kept slipping away, there were no tissues to blot out the red stains on his shirt, and the bread rolls were miniature buns. He felt the restaurateur was sadistically dangling delicious food in front of him which he couldn't get up into his mouth. Feeling personally affronted and increasingly depressed, he looked hopelessly for a napkin to clean his saucy hands. Alas, none to be seen. This is not unusual. Unrequested napkins on a table are a rare sight.

Which is why, when first entering a food court in Singapore, one marvels: "How nice. There are free packets of tissues at the tables." Not so, they belong to the customers who leave them to *chope* (save) their seats. If you want tissues, you need to pay extra for them. Other countries wanting to cut down on trash and waste should take note.

"Does this gondola have Wi-Fi?"

④ The kids' preference for rice over pasta.

Even more worrisome for an Italian mom is that when we do cook risotto, they say: "I don't like this type of rice. Make it the other way." I'm all about cultural assimilation, but risotto is where I draw the line.

⑤ Their giddy anticipation of chewing gum in Verona.

I was told that chewing gum was banned in Singapore because people were sticking it inside the closing doors of the MRT (subway trains), causing the breakdown of the electronic closing doors. It's hard to fathom who would try such a stunt since the last person who vandalized a train was deported (and it was graffiti). Bottom line, no gum.

You can still buy a tasteless generic type at the pharmacy for medical purposes, but the delicious bubble-making type is like contraband.

On the plus side, if you are someone who hates hearing people pop bubbles (Hi, Dad), then this is the country for you. I think the Singapore Tourism Board is underplaying a great selling point. They should proudly boast: "There is the death penalty for hard drugs but more importantly you will never hear anybody rudely pop gum in your ear. Never. Go to Europe for the gum, come to Singapore for the pop-free atmosphere."

⑥ Eliot's knowledge of more words in Mandarin than in Italian.

When Eliot arrived in Singapore she was just five months old and didn't speak any language. Gradually, she acquired words in Mandarin at a much quicker pace than words in Italian. The only problem with that is that I have no idea what she is saying. Taxi drivers are always surprised that she's learning Chinese. But I wouldn't advise moving here solely for the Chinese, because surprisingly there are no schools where lessons are taught exclusively in Chinese. In fact, if I worked in the government, I would look into this. Expat parents are baffled at the discovery. Their kids? Extremely grateful.

⑦ The belief that everybody has a pool.

When my kids have a play date they always bring along a bathing suit. They don't even ask if there's a pool. They just assume. And, because it is Singapore and most expats do live in a condo with a pool, they're usually right. There are some expats who choose a yard over a pool (much to their real estate agent's chagrin). "The kids can run around and play," they reason. At 100 degrees? I don't think so.

⑧ Eliot's teary breakdown because she doesn't have straight, black hair.

My kids were the only ones in their kindergarten to have light-brown, wavy hair. Good during class recitals when I had to pick them out amongst a sea of shiny, black-haired heads; less so when they complained they weren't like everybody else.

Not to mention that saying Singapore climate is not kind to curly hair is a gross understatement. The sudden rain, the unrelenting humidity... my hair has on occasion reached new heights, and not in a good way. My hairdo once prompted my son to rush out of the school bus demanding: "What happened to your hair?" Umm, I washed it... and then waited for your bus while it dried naturally?

But sometimes I wonder. Maybe the curls are good, maybe frizzy builds character. Why is it then that I spend a good part of the morning rush hour forced by my five-year-old to blow-dry her hair straight? Is it because I still remember when I was little and had a rubber band wrapped unceremoniously by my mother around an unruly ponytail in the mornings? My hair pulled back so tightly that I spent the rest of the school day with eyes wide open like a deer caught in headlights. And, at night time, when the rubber band was taken out, I could count the many hairs still attached to it. Good times.

⑨ When they say they want to go to Disneyland, they're referring to the one in Tokyo.

Every kid wants to go to Disneyland. A fun place with all your favourite characters and cheerful staff (unless you're going to the one in Paris). I just always assumed it would be the one in California. They say you can never go home again. The other day, I ran into an expat friend, one who had been especially homesick when I first met her, who told me she was going home for a week. "You must be so happy!" I guessed. "Not really, I'm over *home*..." Her answer made me realize how much time had passed since we had last seen each other. Singapore really grows on you. There are friends of mine, no longer here, who refer to Singapore as paradise (true, they now live in China).

Maybe it's the absence of seasons that makes time stand still. That's why it's so unsettling when a friend does move away and you realize that your time as an expat here is just transitory. One night you have a wonderful dinner out with friends: delicious food, generous hosts, and fun company. But it is a farewell party so it's a bittersweet occasion. One of the best things about being an expat is the eclectic mix of people you get to meet. But then those people leave. One friend is leaving for Switzerland to work at a pharmaceutical company, one is leaving for Sydney, another for Shanghai, and another for Bangalore to join her husband on his start-up venture. You will miss them because you remember how, over masala dhosa breakfasts in Little India, after dropping off your little kindergart- eners, they were a big part of how you went from feeling homesick to feeling like you belonged. No matter how long you stay, you will never get used to your friends moving away.

More signs you may have overstayed

① Your child brings soy sauce to school in case they are serving rice.

When your child starts doing this, I think it is safe to say she's ready for her PR. If Singapore and Italy were playing a football match, Singapore just scored a touchdown. You can pack all the leftover pasta bolognese from the night before in her lunchbox, but if the girl has soy sauce on her mind, she's gone local.

② When you ask your son what season it is, he answers: "Monsoon?"

Theoretically, you know the changing seasons have not had the same impact on your kids' lives that they had on yours (mainly because they haven't experienced them). However, it is still a shock when you ask that question in December and you are expecting him to answer: "It's winter." The fact that it really is monsoon and has been raining night and day with flash floods along Orchard Road does show he has a point. Still, it's unexpected.

③ When asked how they are in Italian, they answer in Chinese.

Even more disconcerting, when they are in Italy during the summer and don't understand what someone is saying, they usually reason: "I think he's Chinese."

Then again, when they don't understand someone in Singapore, they've been known to say: "He's Korean." It's complicated.

④ The answer to "What sign are you?" is not Sagittarius. It's Snake.

Undeniably Asian. At this point, I'm thinking this answer might not improve my son's chances on the dating scene in America. On the other hand, if he never pronounces that cheesy question to a girl, I will consider myself one proud, Asian parent.

⑤ At birthday parties they sing Happy Birthday in Chinese... before English.

At all birthday parties in Singapore, it is customary amongst expats to sing both in English and Chinese. Now that my children automatically and without prompting sing the Chinese version, I can't help but wonder: "Will they ever learn how to sing Happy Birthday in Italian?" Followed by: "Will they ever be invited to Italian birthday parties?" Remembering the huge quantities of liquor and cream-filled pastries I was forced to eat as a child... maybe that's not a bad thing. And, exclusion does build character... or was that resentment?

Uniquely Singapore (Part 1)

① Swimming in an outdoor pool on Christmas Day

Only in Singapore. As I watch my kids frolicking in the water, I make a mental list of all the other things that make Singapore unique and differentiate it from Verona, as well as from most other places.

❷ Parental guidance

No need. Profanity on television is bleeped and there is no nudity. I mean, none. My kids are totally shocked when they watch TV in Italy. And, that's just the commercials.

❸ Capital punishment

Once hoping to have a lively debate with my university class, I brought up the issue of capital punishment and asked my students: "Who's in favour, who's against?" 100% in favour... no debate. I knew I should have prepared more material.

❹ Live-in maids

Cheap labour from the Philippines, Indonesia, and Myanmar. Here, even the maids have maids. Seriously. The wealthier Singaporean families have more than one maid so it is entirely plausible to hear how maid number one is training maid number two. The ideal scenario in Singapore includes a grandparent who keeps an eye on maid number one while she keeps an eye on maid number two. A viable solution for the dual-working-parent household or merely a way to keep the grandparents busy? Who's to say?

❺ School etiquette

Currently, there is a debate as to whether local teachers have the right to cut their students' hair should the need arise. Yes – if it's longer than the standard allowed or if the student has already been given prior warning. The mother at the centre of the haircutting media storm was protesting not only because a teacher had taken it upon herself to cut her child's hair but because that was a $300 hairstyle. Let me repeat that: $300. Understandably, the student didn't receive much sympathy. All students are expected to wear uniforms, no jewellery, and no make-up. Sneakers must be either all black or all white. The good thing is kids don't need to worry about being mugged over expensive trainers.

⑥ Construction work

Ubiquitous working sites, trees being cut down, and consequent loud jackhammering... you just don't hear this in Verona. As my kids see it: "That's because everything is already done in Italy." Condos here are knocked down for being too old (as in 20 years, not 200 years old). The concept of old equalling bad is hard to comprehend for a Westerner, especially one from Europe. Sadly, beautiful shophouses and green spaces are being replaced by concrete. Malls are constantly competing with each other on Orchard Road as truckloads of Bangladeshi workers make their daily commute to work; all the bustle contributes to creating the image of Singapore as a city that never sleeps. And, if you live near a construction site, that's not just a euphemism.

⑦ Food courts

Fantastic culinary oases, open all day and late into the night, where you can eat all sorts of delicious, inexpensive meals. Indian curries, Korean kimchi, chicken rice... all for $5 (less than a coffee at Starbucks). In some courts, you can use a special debit card that can be topped up at the entrance. Forget BYOB (Bring Your Own Beer), here the only acronym you need to remember is BYON (Bring Your Own Napkin).

⑧ Tuition... for kindergarteners?

Do you remember when you were little and couldn't wait for school to be over so you could go out and play? At first, I wondered where all the Singaporean kids were and then I was told they have tuition after class. In kindergarten? How far behind are they? This helps explain why the Singaporean school system has such an excellent reputation. Also, the inordinate amount of time spent cramming for exams (that's the moms), and the consequent breaking out in hives (again, the moms). However, if I think back to when I was in elementary school, my afternoon activities consisted of reading or playing outside with my friends until my mother called me inside for dinner. Not math, thank God. My Singaporean neighbour told me her daughter was the only student in her whole class to not have a math tutor. And that was only because she had left her own job as a real estate agent to become her daughter's personal tutor. The girl's education dictated their lifestyle (the mother's quitting of job, the choice of condo they lived in), there was a lot riding on her test results. Pressure? Just a tad.

9 Cheap taxis

Very, very cheap. The price of an espresso at a bar in Italy
– albeit one where you pay extra to sit down. True, taxis
are cheap, but there are many variables. Peak hours, routes
selected and booking fees can easily double one's final cost.
Also, taxi drivers are not too keen on picking up your child
from school. Even though the meter is running it's something they still hate to do. I have had taxis drive away the
minute I stepped out to pick up my daughter... and I hadn't
even paid the fare. They just couldn't bother to wait.

10 Eternal heat

This is actually a stereotype. It's not always *very* hot
and humid. Sometimes, it's just hot and humid. The
Singaporeans have a solution to this. It's called air con.

A famous Italian writer, Tiziano Terzani, who lived
in Singapore during the 1960s, remembered how there
used to be no need for air con because there was such a
pleasant breeze – thanks to the lush vegetation through-
out the island. Unfortunately, the incessant construction
work is dramatically decreasing any chance of that now.
When there are no trees, there is no breeze. Hopefully, the
urban planners will not allow Singapore to become another
asphalt jungle. Did somebody say Hong Kong?

11 Singlish

So, is the national language English, Chinese, or Malay?
Nobody really knows. The government can't make up its
mind and there are too many dialects to consider. No

bother, most Singaporeans speak Singlish. Not always clear as certain answers sound like questions and vice-versa: "Can I have some coffee?" "Can. Can." (Is that a yes or an invitation to break into a French dance routine?) Had I not moved to Singapore, I might never have known that the word *off* can be used as a verb: "Would you like me to *off* the air con?"

Uniquely Singapore (Part 2)

"Luckily you brought an umbrella."

1 Racial harmony

Chinese New Year, Hari Raya, Diwali... you know, any excuse for a party. Seriously, it's great. There is no other country in the world with this much racial, religious, and ethnic diversity living side by side. On the news, it is common to hear about what it means to be a Singaporean, and nation-building exercises are very popular. I can't really imagine the same topics being discussed on the news in Italy. Not to mention that it is perfectly natural for an Italian to complain about his country's politicians, laws, or government. In fact, complaining is an integral part of an Italian's identity. You can't take that away from him. Whereas in Singapore, complaining is viewed, at the very least, as unpatriotic. More importantly, it is illegal to say or write anything which could instigate racial hatred. When a lady complained on social media about her Malay neighbour's loud wedding, within hours she had lost her job and a formal complaint had been lodged with the police against her. The last I heard she was living in Australia. If only they had thought to invite her.

② Unemployed immigrants are nonexistent

Unlike in Italy, where this is huge problem, there are no unemployed foreign workers here. You can only come into the country if you have a job and, if you lose it, you have exactly two weeks to find another one. If you don't, your visa expires and you need to leave the country. And the rule applies equally to domestic workers and bank vice-presidents.

③ Chewing gum ban

If your kid doesn't chew gum, chances are you live in Singapore. The number of cavities an expat kid has is directly proportionate to the amount of time spent in his home country during the school holidays.

④ Caning

Used to be a widely accepted form of punishment in schools and homes, now it's mostly just used in prison... and my house (but only when Alexander forgets his homework at school). Anyway, if you're thinking of indulging in graffiti or scratching up somebody's car with a key, you can expect to be caned. And the law is really the same for everybody (i.e. President Clinton was unable to get an American teenager pardoned after he scratched up a car with a key). My son's swimming coach told us that he was caned as a child. And it was never for discipline, just for grades. In fact, whenever he got his test back from a teacher, he already knew exactly how many strikes of the cane he would get. Incredibly, he was not the least bit resentful toward his parents but saw their behaviour as fair and justifiable. Considering that now he is a professional swimmer studying to become a neurosurgeon at a top university... who am I to argue?

⑤ Expat haven

Thanks to the strong multicultural and international presence it's very easy to make friends. Unlike other countries, where long-established friendships cause an expat to be viewed as an outsider just passing through and therefore not worth the effort of really getting to know, in Singapore there is more of a "We're potentially here for just a brief period of time, forget the small talk and cut to the chase, barbecue on Friday?" mentality.

6 Very high car tax levies

Annoying for most expats, but actually a great way to encourage people to use public bus and metro lines. Note to urban planners in countries everywhere: if you really want to fight pollution, just stick super-high tax levies on cars. You'll see a sudden mass exodus from car dealerships to train/subway/bus platforms.

7 EZ-Link

Never leave your house without it. Very cool invention that looks like a credit card and that everybody carries. It can be used to pay for bus fares, metros... and even McDonald's (think carefully before revealing this to your kids).

8 Pools everywhere

Seriously, everywhere. There's even one at Changi Airport. Just in case you have a layover or a long wait at the baggage claim. That's a joke (the long wait at the baggage claim part). Just don't expect to meet many (did I say *many*? Sorry, I meant *any*) local kids swimming in them. As mentioned before, they're at tuition. If you really want to make some local friends, the best way is to sign up for some after-school enrichment classes... math anyone?

9 Good manners

Remember to take your shoes off before entering a house, hand over your business card with both hands, and distribute oranges at Chinese New Year. You will be asked back.

Do's and don'ts when you're a kid in the Maldives

① Do pack snacks.

Your parents may have bought the 'breakfast only' deal. There's a reason the Maldives are ranked amongst the most expensive places in the world. Then again, your mother claims she's been wanting to go ever since she got married. And, you've been wanting to go ever since you studied coral reefs in the fifth grade. And, let's not forget that nasty rumour predicting the entire archipelago will be submerged in the next few years.

② Don't assume you'll be having lunch (see above).

After all the dumplings, prawn noodles, and mee goreng you've been scarfing down, this might be a good thing. In hindsight, you should have eaten that beef stew on the plane coming over. But who knew it would be the last lunch for the next five days?

③ Do take the seaplane from the airport to the resort.

Unless, of course, you were thinking of swimming. You can get a speedboat to the hotels near the airport but any photos you've ever seen of the Maldives were taken from a seaplane. So, if you're going to take proper photos, the ones that will make your relatives jealous, don't risk it – you'd best board a seaplane. Be warned: it isn't cheap.

④ Don't drink juice right before you board.

Self-explanatory. In case not, let me just add: seaplanes are not smooth sailing. Think TV show about a private charter plane company that operates in the remote wilderness of Alaska. Only less wild and less cold, but just as bumpy.

⑤ Do try canoeing with your little sister.

It's not like there is a lot else to do. You're on an island and your parents chose a resort without television. Because your mother can't imagine anything worse than hearing the sound of Phineas and Ferb five minutes after arriving in this paradise on earth. You can: it's called the sound of no TV.

⑥ Don't rely on her to paddle.

Your little sister will claim a sudden love for any water sport you want to do. The fact that she is 50% shorter and lighter than you doesn't usually matter – until you happen to be in the middle of the Indian Ocean in a canoe that requires paddling.

7 Do remember sunscreen.

Any essential items such as sun protection, hats, sunglasses, and Oreos are exorbitantly priced at the resort. They mostly sell sarongs and expensive jewellery. And, if you wanted to pay $10 for a box of Fig Newtons... you could have stayed in Singapore. Before leaving, your mom might even splurge on a new bathing suit for herself... one your dad later refers to as her *burkhini*.

8 Don't assume that just because water costs as much as Coke you'll be getting Coke.

Bizarrely Coke is as cheap as water, or rather, water is as expensive as Coke. And the baby pizza is indeed meant for a baby. And yet still costs $20 (that's US dollars not Singaporean). In fairness, if you're flying in from Singapore, the high price for pizza shouldn't come as a complete shock. Ever eat pizza in the Lion City? Is there gold in the dough? The bill will come as a shock especially if you're from Italy, where pizza is still an affordable option for a night out with friends.

9 Do try snorkelling. Just not with your mother.

If someone tells you they are not really a snorkelling person, believe them. What with the curly hair, the glasses, the bad attitude... it's not pretty.

⑩ Don't bring homework.
They'll really expect you to do it.

This one is very important. Never, under any circumstance, bow under pressure and bring homework on your holiday. That wouldn't really be a holiday now, would it? And, just because it's in your suitcase does not mean all hope is gone. There's still customs... no saying what could get lost there. It's Nadi airport, not Changi, after all.

⑪ Do look for dolphins.

This is your number one dream: to see a dolphin. But just because there are posters all over the resort advertising expensive excursions with the tantalizing promise, "Come meet our dolphins," does not mean you are going to see one.

⑫ Do not expect to see any.

If you do convince your parents to sign up for the expensive excursion, you might spot the official resident resort dolphin. Call me cynical, but I'm pretty sure it was remote-controlled by the manager. You can forget about seeing the schools of dolphins you were led to believe you'd see when signing up.

⑬ Do try a fast ride on the banana boat.

Even if you fall in, the Indian Ocean water is warm. Be adventurous. You only live once. When do you think you'll be back to the Maldives? At these prices? Never.

14 Don't get lost.

What's the only thing worse than getting lost on a sun-drenched island in the middle of the day? Your little sister getting lost. Who do you think they are going to blame? Is it your fault she got bored of watching you play pool? There was only so much origami you could do at that kids' club.

Signs you're at a hair salon in Singapore

"Did you say straight hair?"

① They offer you a cup of hot water.

It's only 100 degrees Fahrenheit in the shade outside... who wouldn't want a refreshing cup of *hot* water? Anybody hear of iced tea?

② Marie Claire is in Chinese.

It is pretty safe to say that when all the magazines at a hair salon are in Chinese, you are probably in a Chinese hair salon. When the stylist points to a random Western personality (Beyonce, Katy Perry, Adele) and then points to you, you may not be sure how to respond. "What? We're all singers? We're all Western? We all straighten our hair...? *What is it?*" Don't expect an answer. Just a smile, like "You know."

③ You're the client with the most challenging hair.

No, it's not your imagination. It really is a look of dread filling the eyes of all the hairdressers at the salon when you walk in the door. Who will be the lucky stylist assigned to you? And, yes, it is because you have curly, frizzy, totally unmanageable hair by their standards – let's be honest – by *any* standards. The fact that you say, "Straight, please," does not make you any more endearing.

④ You can't understand any of the gossip.

Bring a book because you're not going to be hearing any of the juicy details about the latest Singaporean pop star, footballer, or for that matter, the client who just walked out of the salon. Just when you thought you were getting on fine living in Singapore without speaking Chinese, you had to ruin it all by getting your hair done.

⑤ You bring in your reluctant son who studies Mandarin, so he can tell you if they're talking about you. They are.

There is a possible solution to the language barrier. Your son. The obvious disadvantage being that you can only get your hair done on school holidays. But if that's what it takes to know whether the stylist is making fun of you or not... it's totally worth it.

⑥ It's freezing.

You think you don't need to bring a sweater since there will be hot air from the hair-dryer directed at your head for over an hour. You are wrong. It is still freezing. If you don't want a pile of pity towels draped over you, bring a pashmina.

⑦ When they say: "Your hair is so curly," it's not in a good way.

Singaporeans are not too keen on curls... frizzy hair is a complete mystery. "How did this mishap of a hairstyle occur?" Your self-confidence may take a blow when they point to your hair and lift both shoulders at the same time. And Singaporean hairdressers are very candid. They do not mince words. Probably not going to win any diplomacy awards. If you gained weight or look tired, you are going to hear about it.

⑧ Describing your desired colour as "copper – you know, like the colour of the sun setting on kitchen pots in a Tuscan farmhouse" is not a foolproof plan.

In your mind, it's all very clear. But when your mental image of copper morphs into a bright-red Japanese anime character, that's where the phrase *lost in translation* becomes suddenly, alarmingly relevant. If only they had not nodded their heads in such total understanding when you mentioned the copper pots and the sunsets in Tuscany.

⑨ Those straightened locks smiling back at you from the mirror may stay behind at the hair salon.

I guess you forgot about the 100% humidity outside. For a Caucasian with very curly hair, there is nothing more demoralizing than walking out of a hair salon in Singapore. By the time she gets home (regardless of the weather), her hair will very likely be a hot mess. The thought of the time spent and the cash wasted will increase her resolve to never go back... at least for another week. Anything to get that fleeting glimpse of the girl with the straight hair reflected in the mirror.

Things I do instead of working on my book

① Make coffee.

My first coffee of the day. Nothing like it. And both kids at school. Silence in the house. Heaven. I feel like skipping from room to room and playing Billie Holiday. Maybe not. I just brought one child downstairs to get the bus in a torrential downpour but by the time I had to bring my daughter it had stopped. Thank goodness for that, and for her no longer finding her pink flute, which the other day she insisted on playing the whole way to school. After all, she's not the pied piper. And, more importantly, I'm not deaf.

② Read book reviews online.

Not only a fun way to procrastinate, it is sometimes necessary to find out what's appropriate reading material for one's son with a voracious reading habit.

A few months ago, in fact, debating (briefly) whether 'Hunger Games' was a suitable book for my ten-year-old son, I remembered the fairy tales I had read him as a child. Even now I feel a little guilty. That's some scary stuff. So, if you are just starting out as a parent, tread carefully.

First off, the Beatrix Potter series. Sure it's a classic, the illustrations are gorgeous, and you fully intend to visit the Lake District at some point, but beware: this series is not for the faint-hearted. Examples:

a. 'Jemima Puddle-Duck': Innocent duck held prisoner by a crafty fox intent on cooking her... scary.

b. 'The Tale of the Flopsy Bunnies': Farmer McGregor tying up the cute, adorable, sleeping flopsy bunnies in a sack so that the skins can line his wife's cloak... even scarier.

c. 'Tom Kitten': Cute little kitty falls into the clutches of a greedy rat. The rat rolls him up in some dough with a rolling pin to enjoy some Kitten Dumpling... scariest of all.

Next, the Grimms' Fairy Tales. Take your pick. And, unlike Beatrix Potter, you know this is some seriously scary stuff. But you just can't help yourself. You probably read this as a child. I know I did. Why deprive your child of all those witches, evil stepmothers, and catastrophic chains of events unleashed when an unsuspecting orphan child walks alone into the woods at night?

a. 'Sleeping Beauty': A witch called Maleficent who holds a grudge because she wasn't invited to the party. Seriously scary (though on the plus side can be used as a lesson on why it's nice to include everybody).

b. 'Rapunzel': Probably the very last princess in your daughter's princess phase before she moves on to fairies, unicorns, and Barbie dolls – all way less scary than a little girl getting locked up in a high tower for years by an evil witch with a high-pitched laugh.

c. 'Hansel and Gretel': Two little children left in a forest to starve to death by their evil stepmother but then lured into a candy house owned by a witch who wants to fatten them up so she can... eat them?!

d. 'Little Red Riding Hood': Where do I start? A wolf disguised as a sick grandmother... really?

And then there's 'Peter Pan'. Notwithstanding the double whammy of Captain Hook and a crocodile, this was hands down my daughter's favourite. Personally I'm no longer scared the wicked witch from the Wizard of Oz is hiding under my bed. I just check because I want to.

❸ Order some of those books on Amazon.

I was walking down Bukit Timah this morning in a dismal downpour when it hit me. Not that I was going to get wet... well, maybe that too. I had an umbrella but in Singapore that's irrelevant. If it rains, umbrella or no umbrella, you're going to get wet.

My *aha* moment was simply this: there are not enough bookshops here like Hodges Figgis on Dawson

Street in Dublin. There are a few charming ones – Littered With Books and Books Actually come to mind – but Hodges Figgis holds a special place in my heart. The bookshop was my favourite haunt when I lived there in my twenties. My Irish expat friends here in Singapore think I'm joking when I tell them I'm half-Irish. But my affinity with the poetry, literature and sense of humour can't be a fluke. I was just born in Italy but really I'm Irish. I can vividly recall the creamy top of a Guinness with soup and soda bread in a pub on a rainy day after classes... but I digress. Not to mention that with my newfound love of dumplings and Tiger Beer I am becoming more and more Singaporean.

I sometimes worry that there just aren't enough bookshops in Singapore. That's what's missing. Maybe I should just open one. My imaginary bookshop would be awesome. As cosy and inviting as Hodges Figgis. Poetry readings, free coffee, comfortable armchairs. Maybe even fresh muffins. Helpful assistants with an Irish accent... too much? Would I make a lot of money? Probably not. But I knew that from the get-go. Majoring in philosophy at Vassar was kind of a clue. On the first day of class, our professor told us: "I guess you already know there's no money in Philosophy. If you were interested in that you'd be down the hall studying Economics."

4 Think how helpful reading those books will be for writing my own book.

All those parents stuck reading night after night bedtime stories to their children should not lose heart. There are many important life lessons to be learned from fairy tales. For example:

    a. Pick up the shoe. It's right behind you, just pick it up ('Cinderella').
    b. When planning a party don't leave anybody out ('Sleeping Beauty').
    c. If you don't feel like eating an apple, by all means do not eat one ('Snow White').
    d. It's okay to let your daughter's hair grow long ('Rapunzel').
    e. Pebbles are better than crumbs ('Hansel and Gretel').
    f. Do not touch a spindle (again 'Sleeping Beauty').
    g. If an old witch steals your beautiful voice, just use a pen and paper ('The Little Mermaid').
    h. And finally, if your grandmother looks like a wolf, it's probably time to see an optometrist ('Little Red Riding Hood').

5 Update my blog.

People often ask me why I keep a blog. I can think of a lot of reasons. It's fun, it's addictive, it beats jogging.

But the main one is so I don't forget these years in Singapore when the kids were little. During the rebellious teenage years, it might help to remember that years before, on the night before Christmas, five-year-old Eliot said: "You're the best Mommy in the world." And that Alexander, from his bed, looked up from his book to agree: "She really is." Genuine feeling of love for their mother or the hope that she has connections with Santa Claus... who's to say?

In either event, better than when she asked me two years later: "Mommy, are you Santa?" At first, like all cunning parents suddenly faced with a child's doubt about the man in red, I panicked. I guess it had to happen one day, but she was only seven. What was it that gave me away? Did she find her old *Dear Santa* letters stashed away at the bottom of my closet... was it something I said?

Why do you ask?

"Well, Mommy, it's just that I never get what I want."

Now, wait a minute here. You think I'm Santa because you don't get what you want. Seriously, who needs enemies when you have kids? This could be my lowest point as a parent (no, I'm not counting the time she got lost on an island).

"Last summer I saw a heart locket in a store in Verona so I put it on my list to Santa but never got it. I know Santa would have just gotten it for me because he could fly there and then come back and put it under our tree here in Singapore. But you can't just fly back and forth... so you're Santa, right?"

Is this a trick question? Do you have any idea how many air miles Santa has?

Perhaps to cheer me up or because we were watching '101 Dalmatians', she made the unlikely segue into: "Mommy, you're way prettier than Cruella de Vil."

Wow... that's awesome.

Just so you know, kid, that's not exactly the type of compliment I was aiming for. Nor is it going to help you get a new puppy. I don't care how cute those dalmatians look.

But maybe I'm too sensitive. To be *way* prettier than Cruella de Vil is really not so bad. *Way* better than... give me a moment.

6 Change my screensaver.

My screensaver still has the spectacular view from the Singapore Flyer – a picture I took the day before I broke my foot. There is nothing like lying down with a cast on a broken foot to make you realize how underrated the joy of getting out of bed and standing on your own two feet really is. The novelty of walking around on crutches definitely wears off quickly (not that I was ever that excited to begin with).

Whenever I hear a sudden rainstorm outside and water pouring in through the window, I get a little shiver remembering that afternoon weeks ago when I was running to close windows around the house and didn't see the puddle of water on the marble floor. After flying high into the air, I came crashing down and heard a nice *crack* in my foot. I was mainly worried about being alone in the house with Eliot and when an ice bag didn't help and I started feeling nauseous I hobbled down to the taxi with help from my friend next door. Eliot sat on my lap as I was wheeled around through the hospital corridors. Two hours later, x-rays done, visit with specialist done, I was on new crutches, with a fibreglass cast on my foot, ready to go home. The Singapore medical service was incredibly speedy and efficient. Husband was on a business trip in China, that was handy. Luckily loads of friends were on hand bearing all sorts of wonderful gifts: flowers, chocolates, and my favourite comfort food of all, books. The kids, initially sympathetic, quickly reverted to their usual requests: "Mommy, can you get us milk and cookies?" But I have a broken foot. "You can use your crutches."

⑦ Congratulate myself on finally sitting down and writing a book.

Since before writing comes reading, an activity which has enriched each day of my life, it is no wonder that I nearly forfeited my liver trying to teach my son to read and helping him with his homework. On this subject, I will only say this: you may have been a Green Beret, a Navy Seal, or the CEO of a large corporation, but nothing will prepare you for helping your eight-year-old son with his reading and homework. First of all, this is *help* he does not want and does not appreciate. In fact, any *help* you give, no matter if it is in the tone of Mother Theresa handing someone a bowl of rice, will still be misconstrued as *judging* him. In his mind, an innocent "You might want to check the spelling of *frenly*, I'm pretty sure it's spelled *friendly*" will warrant an extreme reaction: "I knew it. You hate me."

Lately things have gotten a lot better. He just tells me he doesn't have any homework... who am I to argue? After all, life is short.

8 Think maybe I should be writing a different book.

At first, I was trying to write a book called 'Diary of an Expat Kid' – life in Singapore entirely seen from the point of view of an expat kid (namely my eight-year-old son). I have to admit I got the idea from the very first book he couldn't put down: 'Diary of a Wimpy Kid'. Not that my son is wimpy.

I intended it to be something he would enjoy reading and could relate to. That was the problem: he could relate to it too much. He was very excited when I told him about my project and even volunteered to do the illustrations. That was until he read it. I guess he thought it would be about some random boy that he could laugh about. After reading only three pages and underlining most of it with a pencil (the parts I would need to change) he claimed: "It's terrible. You need to change almost everything." When asked to elaborate, he yelled: "It's my life!"

9 Make more coffee.

Signs you're living in a condo in Singapore

"I miss condo life."

**① Construction work will unite you...
air con setting in the gym will divide you.**

If you're living in a condo in Singapore, chances are there is at least one condo (maybe two or three) either coming up or coming down right next to you. Either way, *there will be noise* (to be read in a 'There Will Be Blood' tone of voice). Regardless of nationality or ethnicity, the residents of the condo will stand united in their hatred for the noise caused by the construction work. There is only one thing that can divide them: the air con setting in the gym. Very high, very low, or turned off... you know who you are.

② Janitor smiles, then spits as soon as you walk by.

Not all janitors smile and not all janitors spit, but strangely enough, the ones who smile are also the ones who spit... and never out of earshot. It's like they want you to hear what's coming out of their throat... and landing who knows where. They're aiming for the trash bin next to the mailboxes (unless they're aiming for the mailboxes... but that would just be weird). The real question is, do they make it?

③ When the Russian hottie-in-residence brings her kid out, there's a sharp increase of dads at the playground.

In every condo, there is at least one extremely hot resident. Say she's teaching her toddler how to walk by leaning down and leading him around the condo. The fact that she is wearing a very low-cut blouse might not seem newsworthy. But if one were to compare a condo to a freeway, there is a good chance that there would be a pile-up. Watching her jump up and down (yes, literally) with her toddler may have you wondering if *it* (or better *she*) is even legal in Singapore. I mean, if you can ban poppy seeds...

④ Japanese stick together.

Handy fact to know in case you ever contemplated moving to Tokyo. Japanese women are the most polite, sweet, and genuinely friendly residents of the condo. But do not expect to be invited to their house... ever. Do not take this personally (unless, of course, you are Japanese). If your son does by some fluke manage to make a Japanese friend (thanks to a shared love of Naruto, origami, or Pokemon) you might have a chance. One thing for sure is that if that child does come over for a play date, he will bring the most *kawaii* (cutest) snack ever – think pastel-coloured macarons.

⑤ You don't always love the feeling that you're living in a fish bowl.

Depending on how many blocks make up your condo, there is a fair amount of looking into each other's windows (voluntary or involuntary). On the plus side, somebody has their eye on your apartment at all times. If your domestic helper decides to throw a rave party while you're on holiday, your neighbour will tell you. On the negative side, if *you* decide to throw a rave party, you'd better remember to invite your neighbour.

⑥ The condo barbecue is like a United Nations convention.

The Italians bring the wine, the Spanish bring the sausages, and the Americans bring the salsa dip. May sound like a stereotype, yet it is an actual fact. I think all world conflicts should be resolved over marinated meat. Unless it's raining. Mysteriously (and sadistically, considering the likelihood of rain in Singapore), most condo barbecue pits are not covered. So, if it's raining, run. Forget the peace talks... it's every man, woman, and child for himself.

7 If you're having a birthday party for your kid at the condo pool, you'd better invite everyone.

Finally, no need to have your house trashed by a class of eight-year-old boys. There is an outside pool and a function room. Just remember to invite everyone. By everyone, I mean even the kid you haven't seen for over a year. Otherwise, it is a mathematical certainty that that will be the kid having a swimming lesson at the same time as the party. Awkward. Expect your kid's birthday list to grow at an alarming rate as the party date nears. You'll be meeting neighbours you haven't seen in years in the days leading up to the event. Suddenly ten kids has become 100. That's not counting siblings. If it's the weekend, there will be parents. Serve alcohol, you'll need it.

8 Stay on good terms with the condo manager.

The manager is like a Mafia don's close advisor. He's the one with the power at the condo. He can find out who's been throwing cigarette butts on your balcony (and get them to stop), he knows which apartment is for sale, how low the owners are willing to go, and most importantly he knows if the lift is ever getting fixed. You do not want to get on his bad side. And, if you're in a real bind, emulate 'The Godfather' and just *make him an offer he can't refuse.*

9 You only see Singaporean kids by the pool if they are having a swimming lesson.

Otherwise, they will be indoors studying. You will point this out to your kids hoping it rubs off. It won't. Why there are so many different types of skin-whitening products at shops in Singapore is a complete mystery to me (and not just because I had never even heard of them before). No need to spend money on expensive products. They can thank their kids' exams for their unblemished skin.

10 Your Korean neighbour drops by to tell you very politely that her daughter will no longer be coming on play dates.

She really needs to focus on her studies... now that she's *seven.* However, it should be noted that when said mother drops by to make this dramatic announcement, she will also bring delicious tea and cookies, which soften the blow. Your daughter may still be sad but it will definitely cheer you up.

Signs you're at a nail salon in Singapore

① One of the manicurists is eating noodles behind the counter.

There is nothing more relaxing than placing your feet in warm water, closing your eyes, and hearing the sound of slurping noodles. Personally, I have no problem with this. I just wish they would give me a bowl too.

② There is a Korean drama on the television.

Singaporeans are addicted to Korean dramas. So forget about the latest blockbusters from the States – if you are getting your nails done at a salon in the Lion City, you will be reading subtitles.

③ Nobody leaves a tip.

When I first got here, I used to tip but then I got strange looks, so I stopped. This is especially a surprise for Americans, for whom tipping is not only encouraged but expected. If you forget to tip in the States, expect the manager to come and inquire if anything was the matter. (Okay it happened to me, but just the once...)

④ They give you two oranges for good luck on Chinese New Year.

This may be to sweeten the blow when your bill comes and you realize there's a hefty surcharge on Chinese New Year (which confusingly is not one single day but more like three weeks). In other words, if you go weekly, you will get three surcharges.

⑤ Some varnish colours bring more prosperity than others.

In Singapore, it's all about fortune, prosperity, and superstition (like Southern Italy in that regard). Especially during the Hungry Ghost Festival, it is advisable to lay out little oranges, treats, and red candles on street corners and over manholes to respect the dead. The dead can be pretty picky too; I've seen delicious offerings that made me hungry just to pass by them. Furthermore, during Chinese New Year, there are rules as to when one should throw out the garbage, when to clean your house, even when to cut your hair. And, you do not want to mess with your dead relatives. Maybe they know my great-aunts Josie and Milly? In that case, next to the dried fish I should put out some cannoli and have Puccini blasting in the background.

Signs you're not slumming it in Singapore

1 You eat cheese.

Let's say you're Italian and you grew up eating cheese every night. Let's say you are now living in Singapore and you have a memory lapse and decide to indulge in your passion for cheese. Nothing will jolt you back to reality quicker than the receipt in your hand. You probably thought you were buying cheese not a Rolex. So if you're planning on buying a lot of burrata, parmigiano-reggiano, or mozzarella di bufala (my personal favourites), you might as well book a trip to Italy... and save some money.

2 You drink wine.

There is a reason why expat brides-to-be in Singapore tell their guests coming from abroad to forget the marriage registry and just bring bubbly to the wedding. And no, it's not because they have too many serving bowls. It's

Southeast Asia, remember? You can never have enough serving bowls.

③ You buy your fruit at Isetan.

What isn't visible in the photo below is the word *SALE*, which makes the whole concept of one melon being sold for $59 Singapore dollars (that's $47 US dollars, 35 Euros, or 30 British pounds) that much scarier. Publishers usually discourage writing specific prices in books because they will be outdated so quickly, but I have a feeling this price will still be shocking for another year or two.

It's a steal.

④ You have a car.

In most countries, a car is a mode of transportation. Here it is an unveiled status symbol since you need to be a millionaire to own one. Elsewhere people boast villas or yachts. Not in Singapore. Here, to denote snobbery, one need merely claim: "We own a car. Nothing special. It's really just to get us from here to there." Sure. You know what they're really thinking: "If you'd just worked a little bit harder."

⑤ You have a child. That child goes to school.

Having children is a good thing, but if you're an expat and that child goes to school... not so much. Home-schooling might suddenly become a viable option, unless of course, your child is Alexander and then you would rather shoot yourself in the foot than try home-schooling.

Life according to Eliot (expat child, age 5)

1 **"Why did you make Alezander before me?"**

Second-sibling syndrome or something else? This morning, Eliot decides she needs to sit on the one chair (out of the possible six) where Alexander's school project is. After a blood-curdling yell...

Alexander asks: "Can't you use your common sense?"
Eliot: "I don't even know what that means."

❷ On a brighter note, when I ask my kids who their hero is...

Alexander answers: "I know you want me to say you." No, I don't. I mean unless you want to. Totally your call.

But Eliot responds without hesitation: "Alezander."

❸ Eliot might try riding the school bus again – after noticing that those who do get to wear a special tag.

Eliot's stubborn refusal to ride the school bus is doing wonders for my exercise regime. She only took the bus on her very first day of school and then refused to get back on the following day. In her defence, even though the school is only about one kilometre away, the bus ride lasts more than half an hour. And since she's geographically closest to the school she gets picked up first (and earliest), and has to stay on the longest. Hello, nausea.

❹ "If Alezander never does his homework, are you going to send him to the orphanage?"

Boarding school... I said boarding school.

❺ "Is God here right now?"

5:45 am, Christmas Day. The kids are awake and running to see if Santa has come or not. From our bedroom, we hear amazement and joy: Santa came! Teddy bears, dolls, miniature skateboards, and Silly Bandz...

"But where's the real puppy?" asks Eliot.

This year both children decided to put only one thing on their list: a puppy. They knew chances were slim but they figured if there was just *one* thing on the list, the pressure on Santa would be huge.

I've noticed that most expats leaving Singapore have caved in. Their children are sad about leaving but invariably overjoyed at the promise of a canine addition to the family: "We're going to be getting a puppy when we get to Connecticut/Finland/England/(fill in the blank)!" This definitely sweetens the blow. I will have to remember this when the time comes. "We're leaving Singapore... all your friends, teachers, the pool, our house... but we're getting a poodle." Hmmm, I might have more luck with a Jack Russell. My kids have already put two and two together. Their nightly conversation goes something like this: "So, basically, when we move, we're getting a puppy, right? So, when are we moving? We can call the dog Buddy... No Sparkle... Sniper is cooler." Some of their most bitter fights have been about what name to give this imaginary pet.

The night before Christmas, we go to the children's mass. It is very sweet and inspired but, after the first hour slowly becomes the second, a bit too long for kids. That, and the fact that Eliot asks in a very loud voice halfway through, "When is God coming?" makes me feel slightly guilty. Either I'm not taking her to mass often enough or we need to go over the basics of Roman Catholicism. Soon.

On our way home, the budding theologian ponders: "If God made everything, who made God?"

⑥ "Is there any place without ants?"

The good news is Eliot, unlike her mother, has very good eyesight and can spot a tiny ant on the wall from across the hotel room.

The bad news is... Eliot can spot a tiny ant on the wall from across the room. "That ant keeps following me," she complains as we wait for a taxi on Newton Road.

He's not following you. Ants are actually very nice. If anything, they are scared of you because you're so big and they're so small. Maybe he's climbing your leg because he thinks you're a tree.

"But why does he think I'm a tree?"

It's 7:20 am, there's only so much mental energy I can devote to this topic.

"Is there anywhere with no ants?"

No, no, no. There are ants everywhere, Singapore, Italy, New York... Just get used to ants.

"But not in a snowy place?"

I guess, maybe Alaska. But I can't say for sure because I have never been to Alaska.

"Mommy... yes, you have. You've been everywhere. You know, before you were born. Before I was born I was just bones... and then God bought me. Right?"

Where is that taxi?

⑦ "Why didn't you *make* me without whining?"

It was a public hospital?

🔵 "Which Winx should I be?"

Oh no, Eliot has discovered 'Winx Club', an animated series consisting of five glamorous fairies with magical powers and super-short skirts. They're so sexy they make Barbie look like a nun. I googled them and found out that this global phenomenon is actually Italian (that explains the fashionable look)... but still. A friend brought over the films and Eliot watched back-to-back Winx... for five hours. Now she's hooked. Just yesterday, I was ever so lightly nudging her toward medical school: "Wouldn't it be great to cure people?" But now she's thinking: "Wouldn't it be great to wear short, glittery skirts?"

The other night in bed Eliot pondered her future movie career as one of the Winx: "When I get taller I'm going to be in the Winx movie, I can be Bloom even though I don't have the right hair but that's my favourite one..."

Alexander briefly looked up from his bed, where he was reading 'How to Design Manga Comics', to ask: "What? Eliot is going to be in a movie?"

"Yes, when I'm big. But Mommy, I'll have to show my belly button like they do..."

What? No, I don't like it. I mean (covering up my innate ultra-conservative stance), well sometimes you can but not always. (I can be really tough when I have to.)

🔵 "My name is Eliot and my Daddy ate a rabbit."

Lately, my kids have started to shift from the whole puppy idea to the more attainable bunny idea. Though we still compulsively watch episodes of 'The Dog Whisperer',

I noticed the subject in their conversations has definitely changed.

Eliot: "I really want a rabbit. I want a nice white fluffy one."

Alexander: "Well, how would you feel if you were a rabbit with brown spots and nobody wanted you?"

"Sad?"

Alexander: "Yes, so let's not say for sure that we want a white one. We'll just know when we see them all which one to choose."

Eliot: "Okay, I'll take very good care of our bunny and I'll tell Daddy not to eat it."

A somewhat scary train of thought, but the girl has a point. Her dad is from Verona and *Veronesi* are known to eat rabbit (you can put that down next to the horse meat already mentioned). He mainly ate it as a child and once mentioned how delicious it is with polenta (Italian-style cooked cornbread). This admission so impressed Eliot that I even heard her introduce herself by saying: "My name is Eliot and my Daddy ate a rabbit."

The heartless dad is still holding out on getting them a bunny but he has offered them this not-at-all trauma-tizing concession: "Sure, you can have one when we get to Italy. There are plenty of rabbits at the supermarket."

⑩ "Can we go to Hong Kong to get an eraser?"

If you have a five-year-old expat kid in Singapore, do not be surprised. To them, this is a totally plausible request.

When I went to pick Eliot up from school today she showed me a tiny eraser that her friend gave her.

"She got it in Hong Kong. Can we go to Hong Kong to get more?"

Hmmm, you do realize that Hong Kong is four hours away by plane from Singapore?

"Well, four hours is not one hundred."

The crushing logic of a five-year-old.

11 After watching a music video with Taylor Swift: "Is this girl in jail?"

No, why? "Because Justin Beever is in jail. Maddie told Katie and Katie told me. Because Maddie sometimes looks at the news. A very important girl asked Justin Beever for chopsticks but he didn't give them to her... so that's why he went to jail." So this is how rumours in the entertainment world get started. By first graders... who knew?

12 The fact that Eliot prefaces most of her questions with the words *In real life...* leads me to suspect she's living in a parallel universe.

If she found herself at a wishing well, she says she would wish for poor people to have houses with comfortable beds, to be a fairy, and to have a puppy. She also wishes beds were made of jello: "So we could bounce on them."

⑬ "I can be a princess?"

In my university classes, we've been reviewing the hazards of gender-specific toys and my students have been writing on how market-driven princess paraphernalia can negatively (or not) influence a girl's personality and ambitions. As a mother of a five-year-old daughter with a love for everything 'princess', this gives me food for thought. So today I asked Eliot: "What do you want to be when you grow up?" She usually answers: "Teacher or mother." So, with a reassured feeling, I asked: "You don't want to be a princess, do you?" With a look of awe, she wondered: "I can be a princess?!!" Not exactly the thought process I was hoping to put in motion. Very smooth, I know.

Earlier in the week, I tried helping Eliot confront her fear of the school bathroom. I accompanied her in to show her that "Sweetie, there are no monsters coming out of the toilet." At which she pointed to a sign which, in fact, clearly depicted monsters coming out of a toilet. What? The wording underneath the picture said: "If you do not flush, the toilet bacteria (illustrations of monster-looking creatures) will come out of it." One small problem: most five-year-old children cannot read yet. The sign has since been removed. It's not easy being five.

⑭ "When am I going to lose a tooth?"

I have to stop leaving loose change around the house. The reason I say this is because of Alexander's neverending tooth fairy money. Very suspicious. If he had this many teeth fall out, he would be a toothless old man by now. He's bought himself a yoyo, a super bouncy ball, a folder and even princess stickers for Eliot.

I caught Eliot looking in the mirror the other day wondering out loud: "When am I going to lose a tooth?" Now when she's mad at her brother, the new threat (which replaces: "I'm not going to invite you to my party") is: "I'm not going to buy you something with my tooth fairy money." So I guess now the two main questions running around in her little head are: "When am I going to lose a tooth?" and "How come Peter Pan never comes to my house?"

Stereotypes about Singapore that are actually true

1 It rains all the time.

Yes, next.

2 Durian really does smell terrible.

It is illegal (and impossible) to sneak a durian (fruit with very specific odour) on the public bus in Singapore (actually hard to imagine anyone being able to smuggle one out of the country on a plane without the pilot calling for an emergency landing). The pungent and unmistakeable odour would reveal itself in a matter of seconds. It is prohibited not only on buses, but in hotels and in most public places. Clearly underused as an actual weapon of self-defence. Forget the mace can, women could just whip out a durian concealed in a special carry-on bag designed for this very purpose. Attention all fashion designers.

❸ Vandalism is discouraged.

Two words: Changi Prison. And, you will be caned. As expected, there is not a huge incidence of vandalism. It's a pretty good deterrent.

❹ It's too hot to walk anywhere.

And, unless you are promised an air-conditioned location as your destination, you will really have no incentive to walk anywhere.

❺ It's very safe.

This is the number one reason cited by expats for choosing Singapore over other Asian cities. Especially expats with children. The thing I find unnerving is how few policemen you actually see and how few sirens you hear. Then again, maybe the drilling is drowning them out. Or maybe... the police are really everywhere and you just don't realize it... the taxi driver, the lady at the checkout counter, the janitor? Or have I just watched too many 'Bourne Supremacy' movies? As an aside, what does it take to get a siren turned on in this country? An invasion?

❻ The food is amazing.

Yes, you will gain pounds and no, do not come here to diet. Most countries have one or two specialties but in Singapore there is an almost embarrassing array of choices: mee goreng, nasi lemak, chili crab, prawn noodles, shrimp dumplings, chicken rice, roti prata...

⑦ Favourable taxes for foreigners.

Recently a famous actor forfeited his French citizenship in favour of a Russian one so that he would no longer be forced to pay the exorbitant 70% tax rate. He really should have had a better tax consultant. One that would have pointed him toward Singapore, not Russia. The winters are so much milder.

⑧ Changi is the best airport in the world.

When you're hanging out at the airport even though you don't have a plane to catch... chances are it's pretty darn special. Kids love going there and it rivals any kids' club at five-star resorts that I've ever seen. There should just be a fleet of babysitters there so parents could just drop the kids off for the day... or the weekend.

⑨ Singapore is one big mall.

That's totally untrue. It's not just one big mall... it's more like many small malls next to each other. And, let's not forget the side streets next to the malls. They're just not as popular on account of there being no air con. Which is the reason people go to the malls in the first place. There is always a new mall being built, which means another mall to look forward to.

⑩ Gambling is discouraged.

The casinos in Singapore are mainly intended for foreigners. In fact, you need to bring your passport with you or you won't get in. If you are Singaporean, you need to pay

$100 just to get inside. It might seem discriminatory, but actually it is a tactic employed by the government to discourage gambling addiction amongst its citizens. Now, if they could only stop the online gaming...

11 Singlish is the dominant language.

The government may have adopted a new policy to make English more widespread but not everyone was told. Even my university students, who speak to me in English, turn around and speak to their classmates in Singlish.

A day in the life of an expat in Singapore

1 Alarm clock goes off.

6:20 am. It's still dark outside, but will be light by 7 am...
all year round. And dark again at 7 pm. Unlike Italy where
there is a huge difference between winter (dark by 4:30 pm)
and summer (not dark until around 9:30 pm). Once you get
used to the consistency of Singapore, it is hard to get kids
(especially toddlers) during the summer holidays abroad to
believe it's bedtime when it's still bright and sunny outside.
Tip: Use cardboard sides of boxes to block out the light.

Before leaving the house for school, allow plenty of
time. Even though it is compulsory to wear uniforms and
simple black or white sneakers, they will still require extra
time to style their hair.

2 Give Alexander a virtual hug.

If your son is in middle school and his friends are watching from the school bus, public display of affection is no

longer allowed. Hence the virtual hug. Best of all, whether it's spring or winter, there is no need to remind the kids of hats, gloves, or scarves. Just remember to pack their water bottle and snacks.

③ Get to Eliot's school.

Unlike Alexander (who goes to a different school), Eliot doesn't take the school bus. So, getting to her school involves treachery, devious antics, and luck. In other words, getting a taxi. It's either that or walk to school. The walk itself is not so bad as long as you realize it will be a very hot and sweaty endeavour. Waiting for a taxi also has its pluses: your child can practise the latest hits on the radio, the multiplication table, and expand her knowledge of the capitals of the world. You don't get to know the capital of Indonesia at seven years old if your taxi is punctual.

④ Nurse measures Eliot's temperature.

After a recent outbreak of Hand, Foot and Mouth Disease, the school nurse thoroughly checks every pupil's mouth and hands before they are allowed to enter the building. Dengue fever, swine flu, bird flu... never a dull moment. After the HFMD outbreak, it's back to the basics. Just the temperature. And for those who think that is extreme, just think how much you like having your child at school with a feverish kid (the one time she doesn't have a fever). Didn't think so.

⑤ Speak to the *laoshi* (Chinese teacher).

Potential daily calamities for a kindergartener range from inability to participate in water play because of band-aids to forgetting homework. After yelling *zai jian* (goodbye), your child may run back for one last hug. Knowing that one last hug can rapidly progress to an iron-clad grip... make speedy retreat.

⑥ Speed-walk down Bukit Timah.

Only exercise of the day so better make it count regardless of car fumes and Bangladeshi workers on bikes trying to plough you down on the sidewalk. Never mind that the walk will leave you feeling about as refreshed as a french fry. Cute exercise gear is a must... or was that a water bottle?

⑦ Teach academic writing at the university.

After a quick shower and a review of students' papers, off to meet the class. All hail the grammar cop. I learn more about Singapore in one 90-minute class with first-year students than if I read a stack of books on Singapore. How else would I have learned that the reason all the boys are exactly two years older than the girls is that they have to do their NS (military service) before they can go to college? Or that none of the students have tattoos because tattoos are associated with convicts? Or that even though technically 19 is the cut-off date, the 20-year-olds still consider themselves teenagers?

⑧ After school

Kids go down to play in their secret dug-out in the far-away place in the condo. Armed with mosquito patches and water bottles, they meet up with other kids and play until it's time for dinner.

⑨ Lights out

Alexander reads 'Naruto' and Eliot listens to me read Oscar Wilde's 'The Selfish Giant'. After I mention my favourite quote by the author, "We are all in the gutter but some of us are looking at the stars," they rush to the window to look at the stars. Eliot points to the moon and says her first word in Italian: *luna*. As a parent, expat or not, I can honestly say it doesn't get any better than this.

Favourite landmarks in Singapore

1 Queensway

Yesterday, I went to my favourite place in the whole world: the third floor of the Queensway Shopping Centre in Singapore. Those who know me are aware that I avoid shopping malls like the plague; in fact, I only enter Ion Orchard with my husband because I'm convinced it's been especially designed for me to walk in and never walk out again. And if we go to Takashimaya, he goes shopping and I wait for him in Kinokuniya bookshop.

So why the Queensway Shopping Centre? I go there about once a year to get invitations printed out and there is something surreal about the people working the printers. Most of the time, they don't know what I'm asking for. Though I've been there at least ten times they never recognize me, and in the past they have even denied that I've been there. It's like stepping into the Twilight Zone. So why do I go back? First of all, I am a creature of habit and I resist change at all costs. But also for sentimental reasons. In fact, it's like a walk down memory lane. Four years ago, when I first arrived in Singapore, I was finishing my dissertation from the University of Sydney. In what were some of the hairiest hours of my academic life, the 'layout' team and printers held my future in their hands as they printed out the hard copies that I would then need to submit and mail for the board to evaluate back at the university. Bated breath doesn't even begin to describe my feverish state at the time. So now when I go back to print whimsical birthday cards for my kids, no matter how many glitches or how many times I can't understand their pronunciation of the word *layout*, it really is just a walk in the park!

❷ The condo

Black-and-white houses are an institution in Singapore. A throwback to colonial times. But along with the prestige there are a few things you should know before moving into one, namely snakes. Can't remember the other ones. I think my mind went blank after I heard the reptile word.

So give me a high-rise condo any day. Air con, pools, tennis courts, playground. Although: there is something unsettling about the fact that, like on an airplane, where nobody pays the same price for their ticket, rents are bizarrely different. Also, the guards keep changing every year, which is allegedly for security issues. Isn't that a bit of a contradiction since they're the ones hired in the first place to protect us? The day after their year is up they suddenly turn... like CIA agents gone rogue?

③ Changi Airport

As I watch my kids grow up in Southeast Asia, I like to
think they have opportunities I never dreamed of having
as a child growing up in Verona. They are exposed to different cultures and realities, they eat spicy curries and they
travel to exotic places. I recall smiling proudly as my son
announced at two that his sandcastle was the Great Wall of
China, and when my daughter insisted on singing Happy
Birthday in Chinese. Which is why I find it vaguely disconcerting to hear my son say on the taxi ride to the airport
on a recent trip to Bali: "But I want to go to Hawaii," and
my daughter answering: "Yeah, I want to see the snow." Am
I doing something wrong? Like not hanging a big enough
map at home? On the plus side, they now know Bali, unlike
the rest of Indonesia, is 85% Hindu, that you can order mee
goreng even for breakfast, and that bringing Harry Potter
is a good idea at a hotel with no TV and no kids' club. On
a final note, there are no children in Ubud, Bali. This is
a good thing... unless, of course, you are travelling with
yours.

④ My house

Especially when the kids have their whopping three-week
(you've got to be kidding me) Chinese New Year school holiday. During the 100 hours of non-stop rain that occurred in
Singapore, we stayed indoors sorting through old papers,
making our own comic books, and watching movies. Lots
of them, like 'Annie', 'Cinema Paradiso', 'Billy Elliot', and
'Bend It Like Beckham'. Alexander's first movie at three

was 'Amelie' so he's no problem and will watch absolutely *any* movie: 'Volver', 'The Bicycle Thief', you name it. With five-year-old Eliot we have to occasionally resort to sophisticated tactics to get her to sit through an entire movie. I mean, what were the chances of there really being a princess or a witch coming up soon in 'Bend It Like Beckham'?

After the movie, I crank up the music and the kids dance all over the house. Our idea of fun. The music is quite eclectic too and can go quickly from musicals to hip hop to classic rock (I wonder what this will do to them?). Then, we all sit on the sofa and they ask me to tell them stories about Josie and Milly, my great-aunts who moved to America from Italy when they were little (back in the days when expats were called immigrants). We usually end up with mugs of hot chocolate and books scattered all over the sofa, reading next to each other. Now, that's my kind of play date.

⑤ The university library

Sitting in the sleek and modern surroundings of one of the most esteemed universities in Singapore, surrounded by students working on their laptops, I read the Herald Tribune, prepare my lesson, and look forward to hearing their comments, which are always more honest and relevant than the evening news. There have been many libraries in my life. My primary school library, where I attempted reading all the books in alphabetical order, and the gorgeous library at Vassar College, where I spent most of my free time during college. I remember one rainy

Sunday afternoon, walking in with Dostoevsky's 'Crime and Punishment' and only walking out after I finished the entire book.

⑥ Kitchenette cafe at Goldhill Plaza

After dropping off my kids at school, watching them wave goodbye, I go to this local cafe, where the waitress knows my name and asks me if I want the usual. As I drink my coffee and write in my notebook, I realize that this was my dream all along. These are the days I will one day remember. If only they had brown sugar.

⑦ Botanic Gardens

Lately, it seems like many of my friends are having family come to visit them from abroad. When that happens

If it rains, no worries, everyone just swim to the stage.

I usually get *visitor envy* (a common complaint among expats who live halfway across the world from their loved ones). You get to hear all about the delicious champagne brunches they're planning or the family villas in Thailand they are renting. But I shouldn't complain too much. I've gotten to see my entire family this year. Even Julian, my concert pianist bro all the way from New York City! When he comes to Singapore, even the barista at our local coffee shop gets excited and hand-crafts cappuccinos for us. It's like everybody is waiting for the virtuoso performances he gives. At the last open-air gig he did at the Botanic Gardens (the Central Park of Singapore), the audience kept asking for encores and not even the sudden rain made people leave... beautiful music or impossibility of getting a taxi, who's to say?

Signs your kids need a Chinese tutor

❶ Your son no longer wants to go to school.

Alexander didn't want to go to school today. Actually it was the first time ever. He was scared about not remembering a Chinese poem he needed to recite by heart. Seems the teacher yelled at him yesterday, threatened to cane him, and had him stand outside the door for the duration of the class. Did I mention my first-born can be melodramatic at times? Probably the fact that he was more interested in reading 'Eragon' yesterday than doing his Chinese homework had something to do with it. Having gone through the Italian school system as a kid, I wasn't overly sympathetic and just answered: "But did you *see* a cane?"

By this morning he had learned all of it. I was quite impressed and asked him what it meant. "Not really sure... something about the moon?"

Over the weekend, he got me quite angry, so much that I told him I would be looking up boarding schools on the computer. The fact that a few moments later Eliot wondered out loud, "Is Alezander going to an orphanage?" didn't really help.

But later on, he bought me some flowers. "Not purple even though they are your favourites because they were too expensive." He even bought his sister some princess stickers with his tooth fairy money. Still, boarding school is always an option.

② Your daughter doesn't like characters.

There are, after all, *only* 80,000. Now that Eliot no longer gets to use glitter glue to trace the character for the word *bunny*, things have gotten a lot less fun in Chinese class. Spelling tests, short essays... learning characters has lost much of its allure. You may have studied Spanish in college or spent your summer in Paris learning French... not the same thing.

③ She no longer sings the cute songs in Mandarin she sang last year.

All those songs she sang that impressed your friends and relatives back home? Nada. Kiss them goodbye. They've exited the premises. And way before fairies and unicorns, I might add.

④ She cries because she doesn't understand what's going on in class.

Well, they do speak Chinese after all. On the plus side, she still hugs her *laoshi* on the way into class. On the downside, she doesn't hug her on the way out. This could be a telling sign.

⑤ You dread asking your kids if they have any Chinese homework.

It's 5pm, they've had their snack, they've even watched their favourite show on TV. They don't have math, they finished English... maybe they have Chinese? You know you can't help them even if they do. Suddenly, you become one of those moms who doesn't believe in homework. And not because you don't want your child to do homework but because you don't want to be the one who makes them do it. Life is short and you're not getting any younger.

⑥ You find out all the kids in your daughter's class have a Chinese tutor.

It's only taken you one whole semester but at last you've found out the dirty little secret of the first grade: every single person has private tuition in Chinese. After your *I knew it* moment, you proceed to book a tutor. Tip: Do not employ the same *laoshi* who is already teaching her at school. This idea, which at first might appear genius, will backfire if your child takes a sudden dislike to the tutoring and has a new reason for not liking Chinese and for not wanting to go to school.

⑦ She looks at you and says: "I wish you were Chinese." She is not joking.

There will come a moment in the life of every expat kid forced to study Mandarin when they will turn to their parent and with eyes full of longing utter the words that parent has been waiting her whole life to hear: "I wish you were Chinese."

Things my mom told the kids (which she didn't really have to)

① "You don't have to go to school if you don't want to."

It's Mother's Day and my own mother is far away. And sometimes it's the thing I hate most about living in Singapore. Wish we could have a cup of coffee together and go look for houses that I can't afford. Ancient-looking houses in the *centro storico* (historical part) of Verona, with frescoes, Venetian marbled floors, and a view. The good old days.

True, she wasn't always great at boosting my self-confidence: "You're going to be beautiful when you're 16... What's that you say? You *are* 16. Well, that's strange. Then 17, you'll see..."

And true, she did provide me with slightly odd presents to bring over to my friends when I was little, "Wait, here you go, a nice package of frozen corn, you'll see, they'll love it."

But when it really mattered, when I became a mom (even though I was an expat by then, living in Singapore and far away from the familiar comfort of home), she never once made me feel insecure. "Chamomile suppositories to help the baby sleep? Sounds totally reasonable."

However, when she comes to visit, she is always full of totally uncensored surprises. Is that a good thing? When it comes to kids, not always.

② "The thunder was so loud last night I thought the window over your bed was going to break – and crack your head open!"

I'm not sure if she intentionally wants to scare my already anxiety-prone children to death but I do wonder.

The only time I truly realize the disparities between my upbringing and my children's is when my parents come to visit. Supposedly they were these lax and super-lenient parents who never forced us to go to sleep early, never asked us about homework, and apparently never even made us go to school. Right. How do you spell amnesia? My own memories are more reminiscent of life in a nunnery: no boyfriends, no sleepovers, and no dances.

And, whereas my admonishments to the kids sound like this: "Be careful, children, you could hurt yourself," my mother is far more direct (and gritty): "Do you want to kill yourself? Look, he almost cut off his finger and she almost got her eye poked out." It's like a Hilary Mantel novel about Henry VIII... only with more gore and drama.

③ "Who wants to watch 'Key Largo'?"

That movie with Humphrey Bogart, or any murder mystery (as long as it's set in a quaint English village). My mother isn't a huge fan of Korean drama; give her Jimmy Cagney with a gun and she's happy. And she can be very territorial when it comes to watching classics on television. Don't even think of prying the remote control from her tight grip.

④ "Your parents throw everything away."

This coming from the woman who actually owns a closet which you have to open slowly because stuff will literally come flying out and hit you on the head. Of course, the kids love it and nicknamed it the Closet of Death.

⑤ "That shelf your dad put up nearly broke my head."

My husband and my mother share an identical passion for interior design. Trouble is, their tastes differ hugely. She's all about frescoes and chandeliers, and he's all about modern decor. Italian Renaissance meets minimalism. And they both have strong opinions when it comes to the fundamental issues in life, you know, fabric and what not. It can get ugly. Those casual discussions on upholstery? Not so casual.

I, on the other hand, do not have the renovation gene at all. When I went to inspect the new empty house we had just bought and much to my amazement discovered an entire new kitchen had been installed, my first thought was: "My God, we've been robbed!" Closely followed by: "Wait, we were robbed and before the thieves left they installed a new kitchen? One with Italian appliances and a Nespresso machine?"

⑥ "If your mother had brought you to us at Christmas, you would have seen the snow."

Hats and gloves in Singapore... who knew it was possible? Or desirable?

It's day three of the kids' three-week winter holiday from school and I'm utterly knackered (a word I picked up during my years in Dublin that perfectly illustrates my state of mental exhaustion). There are only so many times I can edit a letter to Santa. A puppy under the tree? I don't think so – more like a dictionary.

It can be fun as long as your mother doesn't tell them about all the snow that is falling where she lives. Or the snowmen they could be building and snowball fights they could be having if only you had brought them there.

⑦ "Don't forget I'm in touch with the Easter Bunny."

It is especially helpful that your mother (though travelling around 13 hours – counting only the plane ride, much more if you clock the hours needed to get to and from the airport) brings those huge chocolate eggs for your children that you used to get as a child in Verona and which are nowhere to be found in Singapore.

⑧ "Your mother is just like her father."

I recently realized just how much I really am my father's daughter. And it's not just my love of quotes, Russian literature, lists, punctuality, dislike for the phone, morning moodiness, editing prowess, or even desire to read the weekend edition of the Financial Times (undisturbed and in front of a cup of coffee). Well, that too. But it was something more abstract. When my mother came to visit she watched me with marvel as I tried for the tenth time to get through to a travel agent on the phone, finally resorting to the military alphabet: "I said I-T-A-L-Y. India Tango Alpha Lima Yankee." Wow, you really are like your father.

Being the only daughter of a Special Forces Green Beret was not always easy (push-ups were at a premium in my house). I recently saw a documentary on the strict upbringing of Mormon teenage girls. The similarities with my own childhood were uncanny. Even though it is almost a requirement for all expats to live far away from their parents, on Father's Day I remember my father as the only dad who came to every ballet performance when I was a little kid dancing in the Arena, for buying all my fellow ballerinas their own can of Pringles (that makes 18) because I mentioned they liked them, for not getting mad at me when he saw me riding on a girlfriend's motorcycle, for not laughing when I suggested I could possibly get a PhD, instead finding it an excellent idea and supporting me 100% (that would be monetary, yes, but not only), for always picking me up at the airport, for helping me take my first walk after I had a caesarean, but most of all, for being an amazing grandfather to my two devilish expat kids! So now I embrace the Pa in me, I listen to Johnny Cash, I ask the kids capitals of random countries on our morning rides to school, and sing to them the words he sang to me as a child: "One hundred men will test today. But only three win the Green Beret." Adding, "You know, like your Nonno Mario."

⑨ "When I was your age I had a dog."

Seriously? Like they needed any more ammunition when bombarding me with requests to get a dog. The following is a sample of a recent conversation with Alexander on this very topic:

"Why can't I have a dog?"

Well, let's see, you really wanted to get a guitar and then you lost interest.

"But that's because I wanted an electric guitar and you got me a classical one."

You wanted to do wushu and then you quit, tennis and then you quit.

"But that's because I'm a quitter."

Don't say that. You are not a quitter. You really wanted that thing that shoots darts and then you lost interest. The Ben 10 watch, where is it now?

"On the high shelf in your closet because you said that when my friends came over they would want to play with it and they would break it."

Good point.

"Mom, those are all things, but a dog is not a thing."

That's what I'm worried about.

"A dog is different. I would love a puppy. Or at least a rip stick. Or a scooter. One of those three things."

Well, how about a puppy that goes on a rip stick? Or a scooter that barks? That would be cool.

"See, now you're doing that thing, joking. I don't like it when you do that."

Strange how my kids never like it when I joke.

Things an expat kid wants to do instead of swimming at 7 a.m. on a Saturday

① Skateboarding

Alexander has started a new school. This school offers many more sports than his old one. He's doing swimming, basketball, aerial troupe, and athletics. Maybe he was sports-deprived. But to be honest, we're not that sure he's really keen on swimming. After the many laps he had to do to get on the team, his first words as he got out of the pool, were: "I'm going to get you for this." That can't be good.

I have to confess that like most expats who live in Singapore surrounded by pools, I have always been completely paranoid about having both my kids become good swimmers.

On Friday, Alexander had his first swim meet after school. He came in last. I was excited he had competed at all. He complained that the kids he swam against were so big that when they jumped in the pool they created a tidal wave that overwhelmed him. I figured he was exaggerating until I saw them. This kid needs some protein, pronto!

I admit that in part I am influenced by my older brother, who was on the swim team at Yale. But Alexander likes to dash those dreams. "Of all the sports I do, swimming is the one I like least. Just so you know I'm only doing this for you." (Excellent reason.) In fact, yesterday he confided that all the other kids on the team told him that they also do not like swimming but are just doing it because their parents want them to.

Finally, I feel like I'm part of a team: Annoying Parents Who Force Their Kids to Be on the Swim Team. Okay, so it's not so catchy but will it fit on a t-shirt?

② Writing in my journal

Swimming: The True Storie (as read in Alexander's new journal): "I think I am supposed to love swimming, but i just dont, my mom and dad are trying to make me love it or something I can tell because all my life (so far) I have done swimming lesson after swimming lesson I am on the swim team but did I want to be on it no!! can I quit and join something else like all the other kids NO!! so now I am stuck with a bunch of kids I dont know and my mom says I am supposed to "bond" with them? To me swimming is just something you learn to not drown but no you gotta take swimming to a whole new level with the amazing, fantastic Championchips?? I just dont get it at all."

I'm starting to think he doesn't like swimming.

③ Watching a magician on the TED conference

Ever since Alexander got a book on Harry Houdini he's been into magic. This kind of reminds me of my brother Stephen. As a kid he worked for hours secretly in his room perfecting his tricks. Finally, he called us in. As we sat in our chairs eagerly waiting for the show to begin, he announced: "And now I will pour this milk into a paper cone and *voila* watch as it disappears." Then, much to my mother's chagrin and our disbelief, he waved the cone to one side and *all* the milk went flying onto the wall. His career as a magician didn't really take off after that. He did go on to become the managing director of a big investment bank... so he probably retained some of his earlier magic trick training.

④ Starting a rare coin collection

Or something on his own. Let's face it, playing Monopoly with a five-year-old sibling can be a trying experience. Possible scenarios:

a. They get kind of grumpy when you get money from the bank and they don't.
b. They throw a tantrum because nobody is landing on their property.
c. They *really* don't like the "Go directly to jail, do not pass Go, do not collect $200" card.

In fact, I sometimes wonder if my family's own obsession with real estate is directly linked to having had a

TV-deprived childhood and therefore spending inordinate amounts of time playing Monopoly.

⑤ Learning a poem

Alexander is thrilled by my enthusiasm for poetry. Okay, that's a slight exaggeration. This is the new *quid pro quo* scheme recently introduced: before he gets to buy something he needs to memorize a poem: "Right, new cleats for soccer? Here's 'The Road Not Taken' by Robert Frost. You have one hour. Time starts now."

⑥ Reading a book

Last night, Alexander was looking for something to read (he's become a voracious reader and considering I nearly compromised my liver trying to teach him how to read in second grade this is no insignificant detail. In fact, he gets away with a lot because he's reading all the time… I'm that happy, still.) Anyway, he picked up my copy of 'Catcher in the Rye'. I had a moment of thinking: "Wait a minute, I'm not sure J.D. Salinger is really appropriate for a just-recently-turned nine-year-old. But that feeling was replaced with an intense curiosity to what he would say and what he would think about it. After a few pages he put it down, saying he liked it but he wasn't going to read it right now. And then, after further consideration, he came up with: "Was this book like the 'Diary of a Wimpy Kid' of your time?" Spot on.

Eliot last night couldn't fall asleep. I started reading her 'Cinderella' and she burst out in tears: "What if you die, then I'll get a stepmother. Or if you fight with Daddy and he changes his mind about loving you and then I get another mother. Or if you die, but then you come back and I already have a stepmother." First, I reasoned that I wasn't dying, that I would always be her mother, and I even added as a reassurance: "Your Daddy would never marry somebody evil. She would be nice." But this provoked an even more frantic reaction: "But he doesn't know anybody, he doesn't have any girl friends, it might be somebody who seems nice and then is evil."

Hard to fight that sort of logic. So, I did what any rational and sensible mother would do. Put away 'Cinderella' and pulled out 'If You Give a Mouse a Cookie'.

7 Playing basketball

There is no basketball hoop in our condo. In fact, at the last council meeting, the proposal to install a hoop (even a donated one) was immediately shot down. No surprise, as all upgrading proposals are unanimously rejected. So now basketball is an endeavour that *only* involves jumping over a gate to enter the only condo in the whole neighbourhood that does have a basketball court, hoping the guard at that condo doesn't figure out he and his buddies don't actually live there.

8 Listening to Green Day

Watching the video of his favourite song by Green Day, 'I Walk Alone', Alexander observes: "With so much eyeliner... it's no wonder he walks alone."

⑨ Sleeping

It is Saturday morning after all.

Signs you're an expat spending Christmas in Singapore

1 **Going *home* involves a 12-hour airplane flight (24 if you're going to the States or Canada).**

Your enthusiasm might make you forget two important things you will experience on arrival: major jet lag and the extreme shock your body will feel as it goes from warm weather to icy cold weather.

2 **In addition to plane fares and presents for everyone at home, you will need to buy a winter wardrobe for every member of your family.**

Unlike going home in summer, when you can wear the exact same clothes you've been wearing all year round in Singapore, travelling to another country (any country) involves a major wardrobe investment, since everywhere is colder than here. And presents... let's just say that the cute tiny Tiger Balm tins are really only acceptable the first year. Sure they'll *say*: "Just bring yourselves." But what they're really thinking is: "Exotic Singapore, the pearl of Southeast Asia... I can't even begin to imagine what wondrous things they have there and what they'll be bringing us. What's this... Tiger Balm... again? Did you *hear* me say I had aches and pains?"

❸ After realizing the total cost equals the price of a minivan, you may decide to stay put.

Plane fares at Christmas time are usually double those at any other time of year. Not irrelevant, especially if you happen to have children. If you're reluctant to leave them behind in an empty house considering it's Christmas, then you'll be bringing them with you. It would be cheaper to spend the holiday at Raffles Hotel... well, almost.

❹ You soon discover that for your other friends, *staying put* actually means short breaks to Bali or Phuket.

So, you've decided to stay put and you are very happy with your decision because you're not the only one who has decided to stay put. Excellent news as your children will now have someone to play with besides you. Because let's face it, there is only so much time you want to spend on a puppy puzzle or building Lego. Wrong! You misinterpreted their *staying put* as actually not going anywhere. For them, staying put in fact means staying within the confines of Southeast Asia. Preferably on a beach in Thailand or Indonesia. Don't even think about following them as everything is already booked. This is probably a blessing in disguise, since beach resorts at Christmas aren't exactly a bargain. Enjoying the comforts of your own home is looking better every minute. Just remember to call it a *staycation*, it has a much catchier sound.

⑤ The top wish on your children's list will be to build a snowman. (There's that small detail of us living in the tropics... remember?)

There is nothing the expat kid craves more than snow. This is multiplied exponentially at Christmas (which according to the decorations on Orchard Road runs some time from about August to February). Kids may become grumpy when they are told you need snow to build a snowman and sub-zero weather to have snow. Videos of 'Frosty the Snowman' and 'Rudolph the Red-Nosed Reindeer' are not necessarily helpful.

⑥ Roasting chestnuts on an open fire... when it's 93 degrees Fahrenheit... not so fun.

The heat outside will make it slightly complicated for your kids to understand your own childhood traditions. In an attempt to reminisce, you try to replicate those traditions. However, trying to do so on your condo balcony might not be a great idea – unless you want your neighbours to yell *Fire* and call 995.

⑦ Having family visit is great as long as you realize they will bring a virus they picked up on the long-haul flight.

Make no mistake: within 48 hours of a visit from an overseas relative (who has just spent an entire day locked up in a plane cabin with every germ known to mankind), your entire family will get sick. Coincidence? I don't think so.

Thanks to the huge time difference, for at least the first five days the visiting toddlers will want to eat their cereal while listening to loud videos of 'Thomas the Train'... at 2 am. Good times. Speaking trains, with posh names like Percy and Edward, are your new nightmare. Skype is looking better every minute. Not to mention, reliably sunny Singapore decides to have constant, steady downpours so nobody can go out and play. Normally, not a big deal. With stir-crazy kids, a problem. So you can forget about all that splashing about in the pool you promised them: "You just take the lift down in your bathing suit and you're at the pool." Not happening unless you want to get electrocuted by lightning. It may be your imagination but their initial playfully witty queries, "So this is rainy season in Singapore?" will become increasingly frosty and hostile. You might suspect they wish they had gone to Malaysia instead. After they go surreptitiously to the travel agent to change their flights, your suspicions will be confirmed.

8 Your child may spontaneously assume the Buddha position to decide where to put up the tree.

Nothing says Christmas in Southeast Asia like a pine needle tree bought at Ikea and flown in from Sweden. It is only right, therefore, that such a momentous decision as where to place this tree be made by your child... in the Buddha position.

9 You're not the only one who thinks going to Singapore's Snow City is a good idea.

Singapore boasts its own Snow City. I would only recommend it if having ice shoved down your jacket collar is your idea of fun. On the plus side, your children might be less enthusiastic about ice and snow after getting frostbitten ears.

⑩ You are thinking of having your entire Christmas dinner home-delivered.

Sounds extravagant, yet this is what a lot of expats like to do. Well, the ones who don't relish slaving in the kitchen on the maid's day off. Most hotels and restaurants have embraced this lucrative business and deliver everything from the huge roast all the way down to the brussels sprouts. They know there is only one thing an expat likes more than a turkey dinner: not having to cook that turkey dinner.

Fun things to do with kids during the holidays in Singapore

① Swimming outdoors... it is Singapore, after all

If you, like me, hate crafts, long car trips, and anything involving a rollercoaster, then this is the list for you. Head for the pool – yours, a neighbour's, any chlorinated body of water will do. They're kids after all. Tip: Take a book and large hat... just so they realize you're not actually jumping in the pool with them.

② Kinokuniya bookshop

Hours of fabulous browsing and reading. Some people measure their parenting skills on what schools their children get into or how well they do on a math test... that's not me. My only goal was achieving independent reading at a bookshop. Theirs. Now that I no longer have to sit down next to them on the floor reading 'Cat in the Hat', my duty as a parent is over. I mean, there's still college but the bulk of the job is pretty much done. Before achieving this state of reading nirvana, entering bookshops felt masochistic. Surrounded by hundreds of books yet unable to read any of them. Being able to read the books I want at a bookshop has made me a better parent. For some, it might be enjoying a cocktail before dinner, for me it's browsing the Booker Prize selections. Small tip: You may or may not want to avoid the stationery area. That really depends on your disposable income.

❸ A yummy breakfast in Little India

A good way to assess your kids' spicy index. After a vegetarian breakfast at Syed Alwi Road, you can check out the little shops nearby selling pocket watches, silk scarves, and colourful bracelets. You can even pop into Singapore's only 24-hour emporium called Mustafa. Here you can change money, buy gold, find fountain pen ink, or stock up on travel-size toiletries (maybe that's just me).

❹ Go to the movies

Just remember to check the rating first. What you thought was a Disney movie might be rated NC-16 in Singapore. Better not assume; not all movies are appropriate. Singapore has pretty stringent rules so check first. And remember to dress as though you were going for a walk in the snow and you'll be fine. The good news is the extensive food selection. Forget about buttery popcorn, you can feast on dried fish.

⑤ Ice skating

Yes, it really is possible in Singapore. In fact, there is even a new Olympic rink. Allow some time beforehand to buy matching hat and gloves. At least an hour if you have Italian kids.

⑥ Coffee and scones at Ah Teng Bakery

This cosy little bakery tucked away in Raffles Hotel has got to be the best deal in town. Have your kids bring notebooks and pens so you can read the newspaper in peace. Afterwards, you can buy his and hers white fluffy robes, coffee mugs, vintage hotel posters. Raffles is a veritable blast from the past. You can walk through the lush grounds where Rudyard Kipling, Joseph Conrad and Somerset Maugham walked, or check out the suites where they slept and that are now named after them.

⑦ Stay home and watch television

TV gets a pretty bad rap and in my house faces tough competition from video games, newspapers, and real estate websites, but there are some good shows worth watching that might even expand your child's horizons. Okay, maybe not 'Banged Up Abroad'. My son loves 'Mythbusters', 'Grand Designs', and 'Kings of Restoration'. We're thinking inventor, architect, or squatter. My daughter instead loves staying in her own room playing with her stuffed animals and singing. Interestingly enough, my son has pointed out that not all singers have a good voice, i.e. Korean boy bands. They just have good hair. The kid does have a point. Still, it's a good idea that Eliot wants to be a singer *or a vet*... always good to have a back-up plan.

⑧ Grocery shopping

Followed by a stop at the local food court for delicious kimchi fried rice and/or Korean barbecue. Yes, I do realize most of my activities involve eating... blame the children and the ridiculously wide array of choices in Singapore. My kids really do love grocery shopping. And if they're allowed to pick their own snacks and as many olives as they want, they're in heaven. Small tip: Eat first unless you want to go home with half the store. Luckily for us, right next to the grocery store there is an amazing food court with excellent Korean food and papaya juice (remember to clearly pronounce the word *juice* or the grumpy auntie might just hand you a plate of papaya).

⑨ Take them to their dad's office
for a surprise visit

What place could be more exotic for your kids to see than their dad's office? And if it's in Suntec City, it probably has one of the best views of the city. Since most of his colleagues will be away on the holiday, he won't mind if you bring the kids and might even suggest it himself. (Unlikely, but stranger things have happened.) If you bring the kids to his office after lunch, you can check out the nearby designer furniture stores. Don't be misled by the sale signs, they have been up since we first arrived. And finally, remember to *accidentally* forget at least one of the kids at his office. Both might be pushing it.

Signs you're at an international school

① There's kayaking for P.E.

What school doesn't have kayaking for P.E.? Growing up in Italy, I attended a public school where gym consisted of running back and forth in a concrete corridor while the coach barked at us to breathe in and out. The boys were not so lucky, they did push-ups in another room while the coach hit them on the back with a whistle. Ah, those childhood memories...

② The kids' sneakers cost more than your handbag.

And your handbag was an anniversary present. Shoes are not just shoes at an international school. Some trainers (sneakers, runners, whatever) can even be personalized for just an extra (hundred) dollars or two.

③ Lunchtime looks like a UN convention.

If Alexander and his friends at school sit down together to eat, it's like having Italy, Iran, Great Britain and the Philippines all represented at the same table. If only the world's problems could be resolved over a cheese sandwich and a juice box. School is possibly the only place where they don't mind hearing the question most dreaded by expat kids everywhere: "Where are you from?" Dreaded because most expat kids have no idea where the heck they're from. "Let's see, I was born in Kenya, raised in England, and now I live in Singapore."

④ Your kid can't pronounce his best friend's name.

When your best friend comes from Kazakhstan, it's going to take you longer to learn his name (spelling might take forever) than to ask him over for a play date. Luckily the term *dude* is totally acceptable and should tide you over the first few weeks. Now about addressing those birthday invitation envelopes...

⑤ Students walk around with water bottles.

Obviously in preparation for the imminent drought nobody thought to warn you about. You really need to start watching the news more often.

⑥ Kids only see their grandparents on Skype.

In Italy, kids usually see their grandparents on Sundays around the lunch table. If you go to an international school, it will still be on Sundays but on a computer screen via Skype. Avoid calling them during nap time or they will be grumpy.

⑦ Field trips include skiing in the Alps and sailing in New Zealand.

When you were a kid, your school trip was probably to the zoo. Not so at an international school. They take it very seriously. And don't call them school trips, these are *learning expeditions* (as such they are mandatory and require expensive gear). As you wander the hallways, ogling the posters advertising skiing in the Alps and trekking in the Himalayas, you wonder: "Where am I? A school or a luxury travel agency?"

⑧ On the day back from school holidays, most kids walk around in a jet-lagged stupor.

Most kids at international schools go *home* for the holidays and home involves travelling through various time zones. Furthermore, parents craftily time the date of the return to coincide with the day before school starts. "It will help them get over jet lag quicker," they reason, as their child catches a 6:55 am school bus at what feels like the middle of the night. Final result: the school looks like the film set of 'The Return of the Living Dead'.

⑨ **The canteen has its own tandoori oven.**

Forget the new classmates hailing from all over the world, the science labs, the art studios; what your kids will mostly rave about on the first day of school is the amazing Indian food served at the canteen. Their awe and appreciation of the naan and butter chicken will leave you thinking you should have just sent them to a cafe in Little India for their schooling. It would have been cheaper. You eagerly await the first parent-teacher conference, hoping it coincides with lunch. And when you are invited to give a writing workshop, it's not so much the students you are looking forward to, it's the food.

Stuff expats in Singapore like

① Starbucks

The expat loves Starbucks. He clings to it like a buoy in rough waters. It doesn't matter if one coffee costs as much as an entire meal at a food court. Not all expats appreciate their local kopitiam, even though coffee there costs a fraction of that from Starbucks. To be fair, the Carnation milk they add from a tin isn't doing it any favours.

② Chinese tutors

The expat will sell his soul for a Chinese tutor. So, in a way, the Chinese tutor is a currency more valuable than gold. If an expat parent finds a good tutor, you will not hear about it. In fact, he may profess sudden amnesia when asked for the phone number. In a country with so many Chinese, private lessons in Mandarin are surprisingly expensive and difficult to come by. There is no such thing as sharing when it comes to Mandarin... expats are ruthless. They are more likely to share a holiday rental. There are even frauds passing themselves off as tutors on expat discussion boards. Frankly, I can think of easier things to fake than Chinese.

❸ Forcing the kids to speak Mandarin to taxi drivers

Once the tutor has been secured, the next logical step is forcing one's kids to speak to the taxi driver. For those expats who live in a sort of condo-school-mall enclave, taxi drivers may be their only contact with the outside world. Okay, that's a bit of an exaggeration. I can think of many others, just give me a minute... the plumber, the pizza guy, pest control. But certainly, taxi drivers are the most consistent and loquacious. The fact that the driver speaks Hokkien, and has no interest in whether your son speaks Mandarin, is not the point. What's important is that this is a relatively easy and cheap way to gauge your child's level in Chinese. If the kid is barely understanding *Ni hao ma*, it is time to change tutors.

❹ Comparing beaches in Malaysia to those in Thailand

They're all beaches. Wrong. At every expat gathering there will be an unofficial Asian Beach Expert. Some guy who has been everywhere, first as a backpacker staying at hostels and later as a guest at five-star resorts. And yes, he's seen 'The Beach'. Twice. He even knows that it was filmed on a different island from the one mentioned in the book. The Asian Beach Expert will usually initiate the debate on whether beaches in Malaysia are better than those in Thailand. Showing one's expertise on this topic is, of course, a subtle way of illustrating one's travel superiority: "You haven't been to Redang? The scuba diving is divine. Krabi? Can be touristy." An Italian would never think of turning to another Italian and claiming: "Why are you just hanging out at this cafe? You should be spending your weekend in Liechtenstein instead. What? You haven't been to Poland? That's just wrong."

No doubt one of the biggest advantages of living in Singapore is its proximity to so many amazing places. However, expats can take almost too literally the image of Singapore as a stepping stone to the rest of Asia; they end up spending all their money and time away. Not for me the long lines at customs, the petty bribes at immigration, the nausea-inducing ferries, I choose sitting at an outdoor cafe in Singapore, drinking coffee and reading the weekend edition of the Financial Times.

⑤ Organic food

Never mind it costs triple the price of non-organic food, expats want it. Lots of it. Ridiculously over-priced carrots? Not in my cart. In fact, I managed to avoid it, until a neighbour let me taste some corn one day. "Why is it so good?" I asked. "It's organic." Damn her.

⑥ Buying Cheerios in bulk

Singaporean kids eat porridge for breakfast. Expat kids eat breakfast cereal, even though it's outrageously expensive here. I have a dear friend who moved to Bangalore, but comes back to visit every few months. She says it's because she misses Singapore and needs a break from India, but I think it's because she wants to stock up on Cheerios. I've seen her grocery cart. Who am I to judge? Cheerios is one of the reasons I need to get home delivery from the supermarket (and a part-time job). Besides cars, I'd say the cost of Cheerios is as good an index as any for how expensive life in Singapore will be.

⑦ Travelling to Bhutan

Being the perfect expat entails travelling to exotic locations. Anybody can go to Thailand or Malaysia. It needs to be more far-flung than that. The more far-flung the place, the more respect the expat will get. Bhutan... hard to get to and expensive? A perfect choice.

⑧ Describing yak butter eaten in Nepal

Nothing says cool as eating something on holiday you would never eat in normal circumstances and then describing it afterwards. Farm rats, roasted grasshoppers, balut egg? Do I want salmonella? Not particularly. This is why I travel with Nutella.

⑨ Singapore Airlines

If there is one thing locals and expats can agree on, it's how awesome Singapore Airlines is. The only problem is that all other airlines are forever ruined for you. And, all other airlines are cheaper.

⑩ Skiing in Japan

Expats love skiing trips to Japan. Cold, far, and very pricey – what's not to love? If I sound bitter it's probably because I don't ski anymore. The lessons I took as a child were too traumatic. This was before I wore glasses and was therefore unaware that bread had holes in it. I can honestly say trying to ski without glasses rates high on my list of worst childhood experiences ever. Throw in tight-fitting ski boots, freezing fingers and long lines, and you've got yourself a party. I do like one thing about skiing holidays... it's called drinking hot chocolate. Preferably next to a fireplace in a cosy chalet. Now that's a sport I can embrace.

More stuff
expats like

1 India

All expats rave about India. Well, that's not entirely true. Indian expats don't. They're too busy applying for PR. I guess disenchantment with one's own country is a fairly widespread phenomenon. I know that I have never met an Italian as enthusiastic about Italy as someone *not* Italian, whose image of Italy is usually one of a rustic farmhouse surrounded by an olive grove in Tuscany, or of villagers grape-stomping to make wine. Unfortunately, there is no Little Italy in Singapore, but there is a very vibrant and lively Little India. At least Indian expats can experience a taste of home. In fact, my Indian friends tell me it's easier to maintain traditions, religious celebrations and customs in Singapore's East Coast than back in New Delhi.

❷ Barbecues

Expats love barbecues, especially here in Singapore. There is something about that unique combination of grilled meat, beer, and the opportunity of eating outside all year round which theoretically makes Singapore a barbecue heaven. I say theoretically because for some unfathomable reason in a country which boasts sudden monsoon-like rainstorms, condo barbecue pit areas are uncovered and vulnerable to the elements. Which is probably why planning a barbecue for your child's birthday party always feels a bit like playing Russian roulette.

❸ Discussing the humidity factor

Just like in Alaska, where Eskimos have a hundred different words to describe the snow, in Singapore there are many different ways to describe the humidity. All bad. My least favourite type of humidity is the kind that rises up from the asphalt after a huge rainstorm and envelopes you in one big clammy hug. I'm not sure there is an exact term for it but it feels like having your head jammed inside an active clothes dryer... set to permanent press.

❹ Champagne brunches

Sunday is the maid's day off. It is also the most popular day for expats to eat out. Coincidence? Restaurants and hotels shrewdly offer the exact same meal they offer every other day at twice the price. All they need to do is call it *brunch*.

⑤ Boot camps

Expats are attracted to boot camps. The closest I ever got to joining one was buying a cute exercise outfit. The truth is, I don't engage in any official workout regime... unless dipping cookies in coffee qualifies.

⑥ Montessori schools

Before coming to Singapore, I had no idea the Montessori school method was considered the best in the world. And I was coming from Italy, where it was invented. After three months of Montessori, a few things were obvious: (1) Alexander could pour water from a jug; (2) he enjoyed being the one to serve apple slices; and (3) he could sew buttons. Granted the latter is a skill his mother has yet to master, still his lack of any reading ability was slightly alarming. But it is also true that his best qualities were nurtured in that caring environment and now I fully embrace the Montessori method... but that could be because I have been here awhile and have been totally brainwashed.

⑦ Chinese coffee tables

Some expats purchase a few pieces of Asian furniture while they are living here. Others purchase a lot. And then there are those whose houses look like an Asian furniture store. I have never seen a Singaporean's house with even remotely this much Asian furniture. They generally prefer Italian. I guess nobody is more Asian than an expat in love with Asia. You have to wonder, though, what Asians actually think when they walk into one of these houses. I guess it would be like a Swede walking into a house in Mumbai completely furnished with Ikea.

⑧ Watching their kids eat with chopsticks

The expat rarely masters the art of eating with chopsticks. The reason for this is his having mastered the fork. In his imaginary war between chopsticks and forks, the fork wins hands down. But that doesn't mean he doesn't glow with pride when his child eats with chopsticks. Suddenly, it was all worth it. Moving the family halfway across the world to a foreign land far from family and friends... my child is eating with chopsticks.

"Tastes like heaven."

Stuff posh expats in Singapore like

❶ Black-and-white houses

A bit of England in the tropics, Singapore's colonial houses are not easy to get. Which is why posh expats need to have them. These houses are the most elegant relics of Singapore's colonial past. Commissioned by wealthy expat families seeking comfort in the tropics and built with locally sourced materials, the design relies on Malay architecture, using brick pillars to elevate the house from the ground, allowing cool air to circulate and giving protection against floods. Back then, verandahs and rattan blinds were the only relief from the tropical heat (this was before air con).

❷ Organizing fundraiser galas

Posh expats are either organizing fundraiser galas or attending them. Either way they are spending money, drinking champagne, and dressing up in Shantung silk. And no, that's not me being bitter because I wasn't invited.

❸ Building houses in Cambodia

Nothing will make you feel guiltier about the weekend you just booked at a resort than hearing your friend is building houses in Cambodia. Yes, building. As in bricks and mortar. You couldn't just mail a check like the rest of us? Not to mention, some of those villagers can get pretty fussy, requesting wraparound teak decks and Toto toilets... but seriously, how shallow am I to even joke about this? Very. Damn those posh expats.

❹ Bringing their kids to Lapland to see Santa

You may have heard of Lapland. It's where Santa and his elves live and make toys in their workshop. It's where the reindeer prance around waiting for their yearly journey to visit children around the world on Christmas Eve. It's just a short flight away... from Helsinki! As in Helsinki, Finland, a 19-hour journey from Singapore. Super convenient to get to. There are additional car rides through winding roads which need to be factored in, but I didn't do much research... the price tag was incredibly off-putting. "Kids, the only Santa you'll be seeing is the one at Tanglin Mall." No denying it is a once-in-a-lifetime experience (as in you'll be spending your lifetime savings just the once).

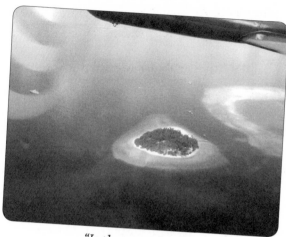

"Is that our island?"

⑤ Renting private islands

No need to be Richard Branson or Mick Jagger, if you're a posh expat in Singapore, you too can feel the unique exhilaration that comes from owning your own private island. Just look in the Yellow Pages.

⑥ Renovating rustic farmhouses in Tuscany

Who wouldn't want to renovate a house? Contractors and builders are so delightful... especially when they are miles away and speak a foreign language. Fun times ahead. Don't be surprised when they present you with an estimate which is so outlandish they smile sheepishly as they hand it to you. But you always dreamed of having a retirement house in the beautiful Florentine hills. And the baguettes... what's that you say? They sell baguettes at Cold Storage now?

⑦ Installing cable TV in the maid's room

Posh expats constantly try to outdo each other when it comes to how they treat the help. Travelling first class? Check. Michael Bublé concert? Check. Cable TV? Of course, how else are they going to see singing competition shows? Heartfelt generosity or merely the wish to win Best Employer of the Month (now there's an idea, MOM)? Who cares? Possibly the newly hired Indonesian helper requesting an iPad mini: "It will help me with the dusting, ma'am."

⑧ Travelling to Myanmar

A remote and challenging location where the local word for tourist is now *posh expat*. Not really, but with the recent surge in luxury hotels, that's a distinct possibility.

⑨ Swimming with dolphins in Dubai

So what if it involves a plane ride? Just think of the photo opportunities that real live dolphins and camels in the desert can provide. Newsflash: The Singaporean aquarium just got dolphins of its own. I have a feeling flights to Dubai will decline. Although: having visited this Arabic gem in the middle of the desert, I have to say it's a pretty interesting place. Here are just a few of the things I learned:

    a. Petrol is cheaper than water. Literally.

    b. Water is very expensive.

    c. Dubai is not the capital of the UAE. Abu Dhabi is.

Finally, a driver who doesn't talk back.

d. The specialty in Dubai is bread. For those coming from Asia, the absence of rice may come as a refreshing surprise... or shock.

e. Chinatown is a mall.

f. Bus stops along the streets have air conditioning.

g. There are pink taxis driven by women that only pick up women (especially good if you're having a bad hair day). Women can also take the taxis driven by men, hence it's the men who actually have less choice.

h. High-speed sand driving on desert dunes... not for everybody.

i. There is a souk (Arab marketplace) that is actually an exact replica of what you think a souk would be like. It's not ironic.

In Dubai, there is the biggest mall in the world, the highest building in the world, the largest aquarium in the world... the list goes on. It's almost as though the urban planners get together once a week, hopped up on coffee, check out the Guinness Book of Records, and say: "You know what would be cool? The biggest... (fill in the blank)." It's an architect's dream location. So, if you are an aspiring architect who loves olives, hummus, camel rides, and swimming with dolphins... this is the place for you.

Small tip: Fly Emirates, the tiny cans with Coke written in Arabic make great souvenirs for the kids.

Random things
I learned
living in Singapore

① A plus size here is a petite size elsewhere.

Curious fact until you realize you're the plus size they are referring to. And you can forget about finding large-size lingerie. And when I say large size I'm really referring to anything bigger than what a 12-year-old boy would wear. And expats shouldn't be surprised by the extremely candid attitude of the sales people as they instruct you on where to go: "Plus size is downstairs." Secretly thinking: move it, fatty.

② Honesty is so overrated.

It is perfectly acceptable in Singapore for university students to enter the classroom and announce: "Sorry I was absent, Prof, but I had diarrhoea." I repeat, *university* students, not *kindergarten* students. I understand it's the tropics and that this is potentially a life-threatening condition and not just the consequence of dodgy food, but still...

thanks for sharing. Or for a hairdresser to casually comment: "I see you've put on weight." Or, if you haven't been to the salon for a while: "Long time not beautiful already." Thanks, lady, but if I wanted honesty I'd just ask my son.

❸ It may not be 'Out of Africa', but my daughter is definitely having a tropical childhood.

I was surprised last night when Eliot offhandedly mentioned she had been told to not drink from the water fountain outside the girls' bathroom at her school because there might be a tiny cobra in there. "We have to use the boys' one... just in case." Huh?! This from the girl who is afraid of ants. I'm thinking she's not clear on what a cobra is. I'm also thinking I don't want to be the one who tells her.

It seems fitting somehow that I am reading a memoir about an African childhood. Maybe Eliot will one day write her memoir about growing up on the tropical island of Singapore. And of her fear of crocodiles (she can't even write the word for a spelling test without shuddering). I feel kind of guilty about that. When she was five, her favourite bedtime story was 'The Enormous Crocodile' by Roald Dahl. It's a children's story but the illustrations of a crocodile disguising himself as a park bench or a see-saw for unsuspecting children are amusing in a disturbing way. That reading choice made over two years ago may be the reason she still occasionally comes into my bed at 2 am, reasoning: "I know crocodiles are in swamps but they could still crawl to our house because they do like children. And we have a lift."

4 Singapore sounds more exotic than it is.

I say this especially from an expat point of view. If you're looking for something more hardcore, head on over to Szechuan province in China. That's not to say there aren't strong Chinese traditions. Stay away from the number 4, which symbolizes death, lay out plenty of food on the sidewalk during the Hungry Ghost Festival, and set out peeled mandarin oranges during the lion dance at Chinese New Year. The list goes on and on. If you spend all your time at malls, you'll miss this cultural aspect of the city. On the plus side, you're less likely to slip on an orange peel.

5 Architecture is in a constant state of flux.

If you don't like the external design of a recently built condo or mall, no worries. Chances are it will be knocked down and completely rebuilt within a year. Six months if you live on Newton Road. Biggest pro: construction industry is thriving. Biggest con: you'll wish you were deaf.

If 'Downton Abbey' were set in Singapore

'DOWNTON ABBEY' is a popular British TV drama set in a country estate, featuring an aristocratic family and their servants in the post-Edwardian era. It seems only natural to wonder: what if the show were set in Singapore?

❶ Lady Cora Grantham would be wearing Prada.

Singapore... shopping capital of the world. Ladies like to shop and the most expensive labels in the world can be found on one short strip along Orchard Road. But unlike say, Via Montenapoleone in Milan, where the shops and boutiques are found along a main pedestrian street, here they are inside elegant air-conditioned malls. There are cafes and restaurants, and in the basement the wonderful, ubiquitous food courts. Where else can you spot ladies with Prada handbags eating $5 chicken rice?

② Matthew Crawley would drive a Ferrari.

Singapore has the highest number of luxury fast cars. This presents a hazard to pedestrians as cars try re-enacting Formula One. Singapore has a city circuit like Monte Carlo and is the only one in the world that runs at night. To the delight of pedestrians going out for an evening stroll. Tip: Walk fast at traffic light crossings.

③ The air con bills would be outrageous.

Electricity bills can be ridiculous in Singapore... especially if you keep the air con on all the time. If you're one of those expats who likes drying clothes in the dryer (rather than on a clothes line or pole), then you're in for a major shock when your bill comes. There are some expats who like keeping the bedroom as cold as a meat locker, with windows frosted over. At night, they sleep in long-sleeved pyjamas under heavy duvets as though they were in a Swiss chalet rather than tropical Singapore. Why not fly to Iceland? It's bound to be cheaper.

In all fairness, my toddler once had a heat rash during an exceptionally hot summer in Italy. Nothing would work to get rid of it, not even the cortisone cream prescribed by the doctor. But after the 12-hour flight on an air-conditioned plane back to Singapore, the rash completely disappeared. I had never before thought about the therapeutic benefits of air con. So, if your child has a diaper rash, forget needlessly expensive and potentially harmful skin creams. Just have the child run around a Singaporean airplane for a few hours without a diaper... the passengers will love you.

④ The kitchen would have a Nespresso machine.

There are usually two kitchens in Singapore houses: a normal one and a wet one. The normal one has all the ritzy appliances, while the so-called *wet* one is where the fish-frying and meat-grilling is done. In other words, all the smells are there. Your cat will love it, you less so. Dishwashers are optional since usually the domestic help is in charge of washing up. The maid's room is usually tiny and the real estate agent might offer the following advice if she sees you looking perplexed at how small it is: "No problem, just pick a short maid." Occasionally, that room doubles up as a bomb shelter. So be nice to your helper, not just because it's the right thing to do, but so she doesn't lock you out during a bomb raid.

⑤ Lady Edith Crawley would have her hair rebonded.

To the amateur Western eye, it might seem that all Asian hair is straight. Wrong. There are various degrees of straightness and chemical treatments are as straight as you can get in the hair-straightening market. One tiny problem: they contain a highly noxious ingredient that goes by the name of formaldehyde, which is banned in most countries. Most expats are ambivalent, shifting from "There is no way I want that in my hair" to "How bad can a little formaldehyde be?" After all, smoking isn't banned on condo balconies. Who doesn't like sitting outside with a glass of wine, listening to music, and inhaling some second-hand smoke? Let's be honest, if second-hand smoke at least guaranteed something useful, like straight hair and hot dates, more people would embrace it.

6 Anna and Mr Bates would apply for an HDB flat.

HDB (Housing and Development Board) is the board that manages public housing in Singapore. If you consider that 85% of Singaporeans live in HDB flats located in housing estates... that's a lot of HDB flats. These self-contained satellite towns provide affordable housing for the masses. But as a taxi driver explained to me, not everybody can apply to buy government housing. For example, if you're unmarried, without children or aging parents living with you, forget about it. You could always try and rent some kids and old folks for the interview but it's still a long shot.

7 There would be chili crab for dinner.

Forget the Sunday roast with potatoes, ragout sauce, or large pot of Irish stew boiling away for hours on the stove (dishes traditionally made with the dual purpose of nourishment and heating the house). In Singapore it is easier (and cheaper) to just pop down to the food court. Peranakan, Chinese, Malay? And, you won't mess up the kitchen, neither the normal nor the wet one.

8 The maids would have handphones.

A uniquely Singaporean mystery is how domestic workers manage to have not only better phones than the rest of the population but better phone plans as well. They must be working for SingTel. This is the only possible explanation for the amount of time cleaners spend talking on the phone. Don't bother listening in: it's either Tagalog (Filipino) or Bahasa (Indonesian).

9 There would be no durian allowed upstairs.

Ahh, the smell of freshly opened durian... there is nothing like it. It's hard to describe. Let's just say, if durian really is the fruit of the gods, one wonders if these are gods with or without olfactory capacity. This king of fruits with a thorn-covered husk has a strong odour described in Wikipedia as that of rotten onions, gym socks, or raw sewage. Though the taste is reputed to be divine and can be found flavouring anything from macarons to mooncakes, the actual smell can empty a room faster than a fire alarm. Fire brigades take note.

🔟 Lord Grantham would not hire
any more foreign talent.

One of the reasons Singapore is so appealing to foreign entrepreneurs is the favourable tax scheme. One of the reasons foreigners are not so attractive to Singaporeans is there are so many of them. As a result of a recent study on population, the government has set out a roadmap for Singapore's demographic challenges. There is an actual board overseeing this called the National Population and Talent Division (to not be confused with 'Britain's Got Talent').

Signs you're at Changi Airport

① You're smiling.

Some people jokingly say that the best thing about Singapore is Changi Airport. They are not joking. If not the best, it is certainly among the top five things to boast about. There has yet to be an unimpressed visitor. The first time I arrived, I was completely blown away. True, I was coming from an Italian airport with an ongoing baggage-handler strike, but still... impressive.

② You're reluctant to leave.

It's always hard to leave... if you're leaving from Changi Airport, it's that much harder.

③ You're getting a free foot massage.

There are many perks in Changi Airport. The following is just a sample: the possibility of strolling in a butterfly garden, free foot massages, fish micro-massage therapy at the Fish Spa, refreshing showers at the Rainforest Lounge, free Xbox 360 video games, a dip in the rooftop swimming pool while sipping a Tiger beer, a blow-dry, a manicure, a free blockbuster movie, a nap in a comfortable resting area. If only they built a condo inside.

4 You're wearing a sweater.

The only downside to spending time at Changi: the temperature. A tactic to deter squatters? The upside: if you are headed to Antarctica, your body will already be acclimatized.

5 There is no question you've packed your own bag.

Even if you have never watched the National Geographic series 'Banged Up Abroad', you'd have to be living under a rock not to know the perils of allowing anybody else near your bag. My kids don't even watch the show and have been packing their bags since they were little. (This may explain why Alexander always has a bag full of books and Eliot has one full of shoes.) That sign warning potential drug smugglers that they will get the death penalty... not just decoration.

6 You're nervous about the chewing gum you forgot to declare.

Possibly the only airport in the world where your hands get clammy and you avoid eye contact at check-in because you have a... pack of gum!

Signs
you're homesick

1 The screensaver on your computer is
a photo of your hometown.

If you are an expat living in Singapore who doesn't go home at Christmas, you're going to save loads of money. Come February, however, you are going to be homesick. Now you're faced with a dilemma: either go home for a much shorter time as there are no long school holidays at this time (especially if homesickness strikes after Chinese New Year) or just wait until summer break. Four more months... should be a breeze.

2 Your browser homepage is set to
your hometown newspaper.

This is certainly a good way to know what your friends are watching at the movies, what's on stage, and if your favourite team scored over the weekend. Also an excellent way to be jolted a million miles away *every single time* you turn on your computer. But if you weren't masochistic, you wouldn't be living so far away in the first place. When I lived in Sydney, which was much further away from Verona than Singapore is, I felt physically ill every time I looked at a map. If I didn't look at a map, I was fine. Happy even. My colleagues at Sydney University had a name for it: geographical displacement. In Dublin, which is much closer, I never felt that way at all. And it's not just because of the Guinness.

③ When you speak with your family back home, any mention of the weather (regardless of what it is) leaves you feeling wistful.

Growing up in Verona, I didn't particularly like the fog that covers the city like a cloak during the winter months. Even though there is a certain romantic feeling that comes with being in a city enveloped in thick fog, it is a sentiment unappreciated by a teenager itching to see the world. The homesick expat, however, would give anything to see that fog. Even if the expat's family comes to visit, it is likely their departure will cause the expat to plunge into an even more grievous state of homesickness. That taxi ride home, after dropping the visitors at the airport for their flight back home, is one of the most depressing rides ever. Unless, of course, you get the taxi straightaway. Small victories.

④ You spend $40 on a cake.

Whether you are seeking your own Proustian madeleine (the tiny cake whose taste brought Marcel Proust memories of his childhood) or not, when you spend $40 on a *pandoro* (Italian Christmas cake mentioned previously, which back home costs $5), you are homesick. And that little taste of home you are craving is going to cost you. Possible solution: carrying back lots of *pandori* with you after your next visit home. Why not? You already bring back Italian deodorants and laundry soap.

⑤ Skyping is not enough.

And the fact that, unlike a phone call, you actually need to get dressed to Skype, doesn't make it any more attractive. But most importantly, you can't smell your mother's delicious pasta sauce over Skype, let alone eat it.

⑥ You check air fares online. Obsessively.

Just because you're not going anywhere doesn't mean you shouldn't find out how much it would cost to get you there. Sorry if that makes no sense, I majored in philosophy.

⑦ You dream about the apricot-filled croissants at your favourite cafe.

I recently rewatched 'Nuovo Cinema Paradiso', a movie I first saw years ago as a college student. At that time, I was eager to explore the world beyond the medieval walls of Verona. But as I watched the movie now, I was surprised at how different I felt and how relevant to expats the themes were. The film, about a very successful director who looks back on his childhood, takes place in Bagheria, Sicily, the same hometown of the film's director, Giuseppe Tornatore.

It's not a huge leap of the imagination to assume some details are biographical and to understand how difficult it must have been for the young Tornatore to leave Sicily. It is very touching and poignant when the protagonist remembers how his friend Alfredo (the movie house projectionist) sends him off at the train station. He admonishes: "Never come back here, forget about us, and most importantly... *non farti fregare dalla nostalgia* (don't let nostalgia fool you)."

I think how relevant Alfredo's words are for me, for my friends here in Singapore, for expats everywhere. How we must stifle those often idealized childhood memories to keep homesickness at bay... especially if they are filled with apricot jam.

Signs you're about to travel home

"Which one is your carry-on?"

1 Your valises are at the door... a week before your departure.

My husband claims that this is just me (and the kids) but I've visited many expat friends' houses before their departures and doubt those huge valises by the door are part of the decor.

2 You need to buy a sweater. It's for the plane.

The rush of adrenaline and excitement after booking plane tickets is the expat's drug of choice. It is time to go shopping: not for bikinis and sarongs, but for sweaters. And don't forget long pants and socks... that flight from Singapore can be long. Packing for the flight might not be so glamorous, but you will be thankful.

③ You buy all the jade charms available in Singapore.

If you're coming from Singapore, people are expecting jade. They are thinking bracelets and necklaces, but after visiting shops you quickly realize that just because you live in Singapore does not mean jade is free. Once you add up how many presents you need to buy, you settle on the cute little charms depicting zodiac signs. Cultural *and* thrifty.

④ You buy many tins of Tiger Balm.

Many years ago, I received a tiny tin of Tiger Balm from a friend returning from a trip to Southeast Asia. She mentioned buying it in Singapore. I thought it was the most exotic present ever. And that was before I discovered it was the only thing that would relieve the neuralgia pain on my cheek caused by an inflamed nerve.

⑤ You remember you brought jade charms and Tiger Balm tins last year. And possibly the year before.

Although Tiger Balm is undoubtedly awesome and a welcome gift, when you notice that the medicine cabinet of the relatives you are visiting is full of it... you might want to bring something else. The same rule applies to jade charms. When the butcher, the hairdresser, and all your friends (and their children) have jade charms you gave them over the years already hanging from their key chains, it is time to go shopping for something new.

6 You head to Chinatown.

The one thing you will be sure to find in lacquer land – I mean Chinatown – are tourists. Some complain that this neighbourhood is actually the least authentic thing you will find in Singapore. What you will find are lacquer chopsticks. Tons of them. There are still some original pharmacies selling herbal medicines, rejuvenating teas, special tonics, and most importantly, fridge magnets.

7 You wonder whether they'll like the Merlion magnets you bought.

The Merlion is a mythical creature with the head of a lion and the body of a fish, symbolizing Singapore. The fish body represents the city's historical past as a fishing village and the head represents the original name *Singapura* – 'lion city'. But a fridge magnet… really? Do not expect gratitude.

8 You head to Takashimaya. Nothing says Singapore like Jo Malone face cream.

When in doubt, my motto is: head to Takashimaya. Located in Ngee Ann City along Orchard Road, don't let the Japanese name throw you (okay, it is in fact Japanese). It is one of the finest malls around. And did I mention the *free* coffee in the basement? Small tip: Feign interest in the Nespresso machines before explaining how you like your cappuccino made.

Signs you're an expat studying Chinese

① At some point during the first class, you wonder if you are still in time to get your deposit back. You're not.

Learning Mandarin is hard. Short of labour, I can't think of anything harder. It is so hard that if my son had happened to ask me if he could stop studying Chinese, I would have capitulated. "My goodness, yes. I had no idea. You poor thing, of course you can stop." Luckily he didn't ask – not after my first class anyway. Timing is everything. And now my attitude is: "If you made it this far..." I have heard him laughing with his Chinese tutor... in Chinese. Sorry, but if you are *laughing* in Chinese, there is no such thing as quitting. Now if you're looking back in a blank and vacant stare at your teacher, like I do, that's another story entirely.

② Time hasn't passed this slowly since high school math.

You're living in the country so you want to learn the culture and speak the language. Well, kudos to you. But if you really want to fit in just learn Singlish. It's way easier. True, Chinese is spoken by over one billion people... but how many actually had to *learn* it with a dictionary?

③ You finally understand what your son's Chinese name means.

Years ago, when I lived in Dublin and taught English at a language school on O'Connell Street, I had a class which was made up entirely of Chinese students. In fact, my colleagues suspected that our school was really just a visa front. The students, who stayed with Irish families, complained about the food, especially the excessive butter and lack of rice (this could explain why they brought fresh eel to the class, a smell that didn't exactly endear them to the teachers). Anyway, they all had self-appointed English names which sounded slightly surreal. The introductions went something like this: "Hello, my name is Li Xiaowu. English name Buddy." Buddy? Really?

Years later, when my own son needed a Chinese name, it didn't seem so funny.

So when the teachers in my Chinese class (who also teach Alexander) ask me what his name Ah-Liu means, I assume it is a trick question since it's Alexander's self-appointed Chinese name. "Soaring Eagle?" I sheepishly reply (vaguely remembering finding his name on a 'Get A

Chinese Name' website when we first arrived in Singapore).
"Oh, no! No soaring eagle (huge grin). Ah-Liu means: *stay
there.*" What? The name my son has been using for the past
three years in Chinese class means *stay there*? And I'm the
one who found it for him. "Uhmm son, about that name
Soaring Eagle... it may not be the cool name we originally
thought it was."

④ **Your children are your harshest critics.**

When I try out my Mandarin on Alexander, he just shakes
his head and says: "Sorry Mom, I have no idea what you're
saying. You're getting the tones all wrong."

⑤ **The camaraderie in class is based on grammar
mistakes and mutual misunderstandings.**

There are only about four people in the Mandarin class, all
expat parents, and we do have occasional laughs. Usually
involving the pronunciation of words and the discovery
that *he* means 'drink' but also means 'box'. And that *gege
kele he shui* means 'brother thirsty, drink water'; but acci-
dently change the order and you might end up with 'drink
your thirsty brother'.

Parents' coffee morning Singapore-style

"I just wish they had more Mandarin."

1 You hear about Japanese-Chinese fusion cuisine.

Whether you're from Rome, Paris, or Omaha, Nebraska, chances are you have never heard of Japanese-Chinese fusion cuisine. Chances are most Japanese and Chinese have never heard of it either. Maybe one or the other, but fusion? Not likely. Singapore is the place to expand your culinary horizons. And a coffee morning, organized by your kid's class rep, is the best place to do it.

② Life in Singapore is compared to life in Dubai. Singapore wins.

At a parents' coffee morning in Singapore, unlike one say in Verona (where everybody comes from Verona), everybody is from somewhere else. Consequently, there will be comparisons and conclusions. Pollution in Beijing, heat in Bahrain, squid-carrying moped drivers (not to be confused with moped-carrying squids... that would be weird) in Bangkok. Over coffee, world cities are analyzed with a degree of scrutiny comparable to that of future in-laws assessing a potential bride. Expat parents are like a convention of experienced urban planners: which city has the best schools, best transportation system, or best housing developments? And just how much better is Singapore? And, does that algorithm take into account the humidity?

③ At least one parent is a Brahmin healer.

It is absolutely true that the best thing about being an expat are the other expats you meet. And that the experience you have is only as good as the expats you know. Sure, there is the new culture to discover, the traditions to learn, and the foods to sample, but ultimately it's all about the people. And because many expats view their time here as temporary, they know this is the best time to try something new. A new business, an extravagant hair colour; you can re-invent yourself and go by your middle name, wear only black, or become a vegan. It's up to you. If you always wanted to try catering or be a yoga instructor, now is the time. And if it fails, nobody needs to know. Or at least, nobody from your hometown.

❹ One mother complains her dog was bitten by a cobra.

The question was meant to be an ice-breaker: "Do you enjoy having a garden?" In other countries, a simple question. In Singapore, not so much. The answer might surprise you (I'm guessing almost as much as it surprised her dog). And for the record, this is exactly why I don't have a garden. Do we live in the English Cotswolds? I don't think so. Theoretically, we would all like a garden... just not one *that will kill us*. One of my expat friends kindly keeps us updated via photos posted on her social network of the reptiles she finds slithering around her black-and-white house. I usually get to see them right before bedtime. Thank you for that.

❺ The main topic is the Mandarin programme at school.

International teachers, professional swim coaches, and enviable theatre. Not too much to complain about at international schools (except for the fees, of course). Oh wait, there's the Chinese. Expat parents can always find something to complain about the Mandarin program. And usually that there's not enough of it. Expat parents expect one thing when it comes to Chinese: fluency.

In transit: 24 hours in Singapore

> **WARNING!**
> This entry is not funny and may
> even provide useful information

➊ 8:30 a.m. Coffee at the Polo Club

This list is dedicated to those travellers who may be just on a layover and can only spend one day in Singapore. Here is a small sample of the many special things to do. Any of these will leave an indelible memory of Singapore; however, with comfortable shoes and a little energy, it is also possible to do them all.

First off, coffee at the Polo Club. Unlike other clubs in Singapore, membership is not required at this discreet club full of colonial charm. This is not a publicized bit of information, which is just as well. If you're lucky, you can enjoy a glass of wine on the verandah overlooking the polo field while a match is going on. If not, you can let your kids walk over to the stables and give carrots to the horses. If you're not a cat-lover, beware of those pesky cats following you.

🟢 10:00 a.m. Shopping on Orchard Road

Singapore is viewed by many as the shopping capital of the world, and if you go to Takashimaya at exactly 10 am when the store opens, each member of staff will bow as you enter through the doors. Prices are still high but the fact that you are briefly treated like royalty definitely improves your disposition.

🟢 12:30 p.m. Prawn noodles at Food Republic

There is a dazzling array of food at the aptly named Food Republic (located at Wisma Atria, on Orchard Road) but one vendor is clearly superior: the stall serving a delicious, piping-hot plate of prawn noodles on an *opeh* leaf (a brown, dried palm leaf). You'll recognize it from the long line of customers patiently waiting for their fresh noodles cooked on the spot.

🟢 2:00 p.m. Luge at Sentosa

Fun for adults and kids alike. You can enjoy the gorgeous views of Sentosa (a popular island resort in Singapore) as you speed downhill. If you're feeling adventurous, you can jump into the water at Palawan Beach. As long as you ignore the many oil tankers, you'll feel like you're on an exotic beach under swaying palm trees.

⑤ 4:00 p.m. High tea at the Fullerton Hotel

Housed in the old General Post Office building, the Fullerton Hotel is one of the most impressive colonial buildings in Singapore. The facade and luxurious interior will transport you to another age. And the multi-tiered stand of dainty cakes and exquisite sandwiches is not too shabby either.

⑥ 6:30 p.m. Dinner at a Peranakan restaurant

Peranakans are descendants of early Chinese migrants who settled in Singapore and married local Malays. One of their most significant contributions is culinary. A classic example of their delicious fusion cuisine is laksa (a spicy noodle soup). If you have an addictive personality, avoid it.

⑦ 8:00 p.m. Singapore Sling at Raffles Hotel

Raffles Hotel, established in 1887 by two Armenian brothers, is Singapore's most venerable institution. It's a tradition to have a Singapore Sling (the cocktail invented here) at the Long Bar at Raffles. According to a local legend, this is where the last tiger in Singapore was shot. Expect to walk on peanut shells on the way out as patrons are encouraged to throw the shells on the ground (voted Least Popular Joint by cleaners).

⑧ 9:30 p.m. Night Safari at the Singapore Zoo

Most zoos are depressing places because of the cages. Not the Singapore Zoo. That's because you won't find any cages here. No joke. And if you go there at night and see the

Halloween-themed park (possibly banned now), your child could easily be traumatized for life. On the other hand, if you just flew in from another country and want him to get over jet lag quickly this could be just the thing. This zoo is truly unique. And that was even before the giant pandas from China, Kai Kai and Jia Jia, arrived.

⑨ 11:30 p.m. Nightcap at 1-Altitude

For the best view in town, head over to the bar 1-Altitude. Drinks are pricey but the view is worth it. Especially if it's your only night in town. And someone else is paying.

Signs you're at a grocery store in Singapore

① They sell abalone.

What exactly is abalone? And why is it canned? Literally sea snails that were once a rare delicacy and luxury item served at special banquets, abalone is now sold canned at grocery stores. You can buy the kind seasoned with chili, pink, or original. They are all very expensive and displayed behind locked glass windows.

② They have hand sanitizer at the checkout counter.

In Singapore, even if you forget to carry hand sanitizer in your bag, you will find it everywhere: at school gates, fast food restaurants, checkout counters, department store entrances.

❸ They take your cash with both hands.
Literally.

Whether it's cash, a credit card, or a receipt, the polite way to hand someone something in Singapore is using both hands. I now find myself handing pop quizzes to my students with both hands. It remains unpleasant, but I'm hoping it softens the blow.

❹ Berries cost a fortune.

Strawberries, raspberries, blueberries... it would be less expensive to buy a plot of land and just grow them yourself. The fact that this fruit is flown in from California or Japan helps explain the price. You're paying the berry's airfare, and it's not flying economy. If you want local and inexpensive fruit then you should go to the wet market. It's just called *wet*, they don't actually throw water on you when you're there.

❺ There is an entire aisle devoted
to rice crackers.

Traditionally a Japanese snack, rice crackers are very popular in Singapore, with endless varieties: tiger prawn, black bean with soy sauce, barbecue seaweed...

❻ Mosquito patches are next to the Tic Tacs.

It might be optimistic to think a non-toxic, citronella-based Hello Kitty skin patch will ward off the deadly dengue fever-carrying Aedes mosquito... but in Singapore that's the plan.

⑦ They sell Essence of Chicken energy drinks.

Who wouldn't like a refreshing, invigorating Essence of Chicken energy drink? I know I would. Essential for any marathon runner, this supplement drink will help keep your mind alert. Here it is considered a must for all primary school students, promising to help deliver better exam results. And if something guarantees better results, Singaporeans are willing to eat/drink/do almost anything. Although: even those who advertise Essence of Chicken usually open their pitch with: "Once you get over its awful taste, it delivers quite a punch."

⑧ The air con will give you pneumonia.

The freezing temperature isn't really conducive to browsing. The last time I felt this cold I was in an open-air market in Moscow... in December. Only there were fewer drafts. You'd better know what brand of waffles you're buying and don't even think of asking the kids to choose their favourite cookies. Just grab the groceries, pay, and get out of there.

⑨ There is a dizzying variety of chili sauces.

In a country where chili makes or breaks a hawker stall, sauce is not something to be taken lightly. Taste, texture, whether it's made from scratch. There are many varieties: oyster omelette chili sauce, chili sauce for pig's organ soup, light soy sauce with chili, perfect for fish ball soup, and Teochew porridge chili sauce. A supermarket in Singapore is chili heaven.

⑩ You can buy bird's nest face masks.

Where else can you do that? If bird's nest extract has beneficial properties when you drink it, why not spread it all over your face?

⑪ It's open every day.

Except for Chinese New Year, which usually falls at the end of January. In fact, most restaurants, food stalls, hairdressers, and schools are closed. Expect mountains of mandarins, plenty of red and gold (auspicious colours), hanging salted poultry (the way meat was preserved before refrigeration), and characters symbolizing good luck in the lead-up to the big day.

Stuff expats find somewhat disconcerting about Singapore

① Ninja aunties who cut queues

Forget Navy Seals and Green Berets, if the CIA wants to catch terrorists in a timely fashion, it should start using this local stealth force. Experts in speed and cunning, Singaporean aunties can be found primarily at grocery stores, on school buses, or serving as casual vigilantes on playgrounds.

② Surprise rainstorms

It is 100% guaranteed that there will be a torrential downpour the minute you finish hanging your laundry outside. The natural corollary to this is that you'd have to be a freakishly optimistic kind of person to hang out laundry in the first place. Don't feel badly, that bright shining sun would have fooled anybody. You just shouldn't have gotten distracted while your clothes were outside.

❸ Mould

Here in Singapore, even the mould has mould. Prepare to spend hours researching the topic. You might surprisingly become the condo resident expert on mould and on how to get rid of it. Your parents may have envisioned you one day accepting a Nobel Prize: "I would like to thank the committee..." Instead, you are indicated as the go-to mould person on your building communication board. Dream big.

❹ Crazy drivers

If you think the drivers in Singapore are crazy, you'd better not drive in Italy. And definitely do not venture south of Florence. You might want to rethink that car rental you were planning on getting this summer. In Naples, following traffic lights is optional and pedestrians cross quickly whether it's green or red. I say this as a non-driver... a scared one.

❺ Perfume is not advisable

One word: mosquitoes. I am a perfume person. Singapore is not the best place to indulge in this passion. It can have consequences. On the plus side, if the weekly mosquito fogging doesn't kill you with its toxic fumes, it can work as an ad hoc scent. Granted it's an acquired taste but at least the mosquitoes don't like it.

❻ Speed of construction work

Every summer trip to Europe, it seems the same two buildings are still being built. Frankfurt Airport? Yes, you.

Enough already with that extension you've been adding for the last four years. Just ship the entire thing to Singapore. They'll finish it in a fortnight and ship it back.

7 Bubble tea

What exactly is bubble tea? What are those multicoloured ball-shaped things at the bottom of the cup? And more importantly, can they choke you if you accidentally suck one up your straw?

8 Soup is not just soup here. It's a drink.

Coke? Water? Wine? No, thanks, I'll just have a bowl of soup with my meal. Sure, it's healthy, but can you carry a bottle of soup on a long hike? Or to the gym? I don't think so.

Signs there's a hazardous haze in Singapore

1 **Beijing here: "Who's laughing now?"**

This is what Singapore looks like today. And it smells like a bonfire out there – minus the marshmallows. Hazing season has begun (to not be confused with first-year initiation rites at a fraternity), and it's not pretty. When expats are booking tickets to Hong Kong to get some fresh air, you know things are bleak.

❷ Indonesia voted Least Popular Neighbour.

Illegal fires (the so-called slash-and-burn technique used on farms to make room for new crops) from the neighbouring Indonesian island of Sumatra are causing the thick smoke. Tensions are high. Requests for beef rendang have plummeted. In America they say: "Don't mess with Texas." In Southeast Asia, it's: "Don't mess with Indonesia." Size matters.

❸ Outside looks like the film set of 'Apocalypse Now'.

Francis Ford Coppola would have killed to have a natural setting like this for his masterpiece 'Apocalypse Now'. And this was probably what Kurtz from Conrad's 'Heart of Darkness' had in mind when he murmured: "The horror, the horror!" – certainly not the beautiful green gardens of the Raffles Hotel, where the author liked to sojourn while in Singapore.

❹ No problem getting a taxi.

There is always a silver lining. I really can't blame anyone but myself. I did say I missed the fog in Verona... be careful what you wish for.

❺ Children are encouraged to stay indoors and play video games.

The haze, and debilitating air, have prompted the Singapore government to issue a warning for children and the elderly to stay indoors. Kids finally have the justification they needed to spend hours on Minecraft. The elderly just think they've misplaced their glasses.

⑥ All picnic items are on sale.

Haze has pushed its way to the top as best reason to *not* rush out and have an open-air picnic. (Humidity and rainstorms, suddenly outranked, are both feeling dejected and have vowed revenge.)

⑦ The PSI (Pollutant Standards Index) is followed more closely than the Nikkei index.

A PSI over 100 is unhealthy. Yesterday it hit 401 – highest ever recorded in Singapore. Forget the usual pleasantries, expats now greet each other with wild eyes and urgent updates: "What's the latest PSI?"

⑧ Somewhere in Sumatra, there is a farmer without internet saying: "I think we're getting away with this"...

Expat's Bucket List

❶ Eat a durian.

So it has a pungent smell… don't be a sissy, eat a durian. You are not required to do military service, the least you could do is try the national fruit. You won't regret it. There's a reason people say durian smells like hell but tastes like heaven.

❷ Have ice cream in bread.

You know you want to. And after you do, you'll wonder how you were satisfied all these years with sugary waffle cones. Ice cream in bread… does it come with ciabatta?

❸ Drink coffee from a bag.

For the first few months in Singapore, you wonder why so many people are carrying around coloured fluid in transparent bags. The kind usually hanging from an IV pole. Were they just discharged from the hospital? Nope, it's just coffee in a bag. I wonder how a Frappuccino would taste from a bag?

④ Order laksa for breakfast.

Forget coffee and muffins, have a nice, hot bowl of laksa instead. Or if you want to be truly hardcore, order fishball soup. Because nothing says breakfast like fishball soup. So what if it's 10 am? Eat like a Singaporean. Look how skinny they are... that should be incentive enough.

⑤ Spend an entire day at Sentosa without getting heat stroke.

This is a tough one. The popular island resort is like Disneyland, Miami, and Las Vegas all rolled into one. It just happens to be the hottest place in all of Singapore. Forget to drink water and you could die. It's happened. Spend an entire day there and you're guaranteed to need mineral salts just to get out of bed the next day to ward off deadly dehydration effects. Kids seem to enjoy it and it is relatively inexpensive... sorry did I say relatively inexpensive? I meant to say ridiculously expensive. If you do go, the only person happier than your kids will be Visa.

⑥ Do morning tai chi at the Botanic Gardens.

Join the silent army of little old people, who are fitter at 80 than you were at 20... you won't feel inadequate or out of shape. Right. You will be doing something good for your body and soul. Just ignore the life-threatening electric storms, the crazy kids trying to hit you with a frisbee,

and the rabid unleashed dogs lunging for your neck and...
relax.

⑦ Learn the difference between Hokkien and Teochew.

Never mistake one Chinese dialect for another. That's like
mistaking French for German. There will be unpleasant
repercussions. Instead, you could begin all conversations
with the savvy, much-loved ice-breaker: "Is that Hokkien?"
Of course, if the sentence you are referring to was actually spoken in English, you might not get the admiring
response you were hoping for. But nobody can say you
didn't try.

⑧ Sit through a Chinese opera.

Pleasant? Yes, if you compare it to getting a stubbed toe. Or
if you consider three straight hours of crossdressing, dire
story lines, and falsetto singing in a language you don't
understand a treat. Come to think of it: you can get that
at an Italian opera.

⑨ Get a fish pedicure.

Sure, why not? Just throw in a piranha and we'll call it a
night. I don't think so. As it is, I'm the least popular client
at the nail salon because of my freakishly ticklish feet. Add
the nibbling flesh-eating fish and it wouldn't be pretty.
I'd rather my fish in an aquarium or in a frying pan with
lemon and olive oil, thank you very much.

10 Take a bumboat to Pulau Ubin.

Venture out to see the way kampong life in Singapore used to be. Tip: Spraying yourself with Tiger Balm to keep away potential mosquitoes will not endear you to the other passengers on the boat. And, hurry up, there are rumours that this heritage treasure has a limited lifetime because of its prime real estate potential.

*   *   *

THE FACT THAT I have yet to cross even one of these items off my bucket list is proof that there is a lot left to experience here in Singapore. If you have your own bucket list, you'd better get started, because, in the words of John Lennon: "Life is what happens to you while you're busy making other plans." Goodbye for now, I need to buy some durian.

About the author

JENNIFER GARGIULO is an author, university lecturer and blogger. After a degree in philosophy at Vassar College and a PhD in literature at the University of Sydney, she decided it was time to embark on an even more lucrative career path and wisely chose creative writing. Originally from Verona, Italy, she has lived in Singapore for the past seven years with her husband, Michele, and two children, Alexander and Eliot, and spends most of her free time drinking coffee, updating her blog, and eating macarons.